D0353672

Brief Lives.
Leo Tolstoy

Brief Lives:
Leo Tolstoy

Anthony Briggs

ET REMOTISSIMA PROPE

Brief Lives
Published by Hesperus Press Limited
4 Rickett Street, London sw6 1ru
www.hesperuspress.com

First published by Hesperus Press Limited, 2010

Designed and typeset by Fraser Muggeridge studio
Printed in Jordan by Jordan National Press

isbn: 978-1-84391-911-7

Contents

It is an awesome business that there should have been a Tolstoy
on this small planet. Each one of us is the richer for it.

George Steiner

Can it be that Schopenhauer and I are the only ones bright enough
to appreciate the senseless evil of life?

Leo Tolstoy, *A Confession*

The 'Brief Life' of a Colossus

One of the greatest achievements in world publishing was accomplished in the twentieth century by a team of Soviet scholars working for three decades on the *Complete Works* of Leo Nikolayevich Tolstoy (1928–58), which ran to *ninety* large volumes. It is in such massive terms that the scope and significance of this master writer and his works have to be weighed. Everything about Tolstoy looms large. Just as the greatest of philosophers, Plato, was nicknamed after his massiveness (*platys* means broad), Tolstoy also inherited a name that implies bulk (*tolstyy* meaning fat, thick or heavy), and even his forename is leonine. He was a big man, tall and strong. In his youth he wanted to become the strongest man in the world, and took physical exercise to bring that about. In the Caucasus he vied with the Cossacks in feats of horsemanship. In later years he could lift over a hundredweight with one hand, and swing a scythe all day with the peasants. He could work for eight to ten hours at a stretch at his desk, and keep this up for days and weeks on end. His appetite for living and learning were colossal; his intellect, uncorrupted by much formal education, was formidable. He could knock off Ancient Greek in a few weeks, and ten years later repeat the trick with Hebrew. Even his many mistakes were enormous. A vigorous sex drive caused him endless problems, not least with his long-suffering wife. He lived a long life, fathering thirteen children and dying in his eighty-third year, celebrated for having written, by common acknowledgement, the biggest and best novel in the world. By that time he was the most famous man in Russia, and also recognised across the globe as a titan of moral and spiritual leadership, described by some as 'the conscience of the world'. A recent commentator, Paul Johnson, has called him 'God's Elder Brother'; the title may have been bestowed ironically, but Tolstoy remains almost the only writer to whom it could have been applied. For Leo Tolstoy, no dabbler in lyrics or sketches, the only scale was Gargantuan.

Unfortunately, magnitude applies not only to the great man's qualities, but also to his defects of character. He was impossible to live with, largely because of a burning impatience with everyone and everything. From an early age he suffered from a kind of spiritual anguish caused by an increasing awareness of how imperfect the world is. He did not spare himself in this: the toughest thing he had to deal with as he grew up was the knowledge that he could see his own faults of character, and could do nothing about them. He plunged off into one direction after another in the vain belief that he could find a way of improving things for himself and for humanity at large, only to reap one disappointment after another. (Pierre Bezukhov in *War and Peace* does something similar until he comes to his senses.) As the years went by, apart from a short time in the 1860s when he was newly married, he found no happiness, but was pursued by his demon of dissatisfaction, to which he soon added a dread of his own mortality that blighted the second half of his life.

An interesting feature of those four decades is his choice of companions on the way to dusty death. Disillusioned by women, not least by his poor wife, he turned for inspiration and guidance to two appalling male figures. The first was the German philosopher Arthur Schopenhauer, unassailable holder of the world heavyweight title in pessimism. The second was a fanatical born-again-Christian aristocrat, Vladimir Chertkov, who began as a Tolstoyan disciple, became his confidant and self-appointed business manager, and ended up dominating him psychologically and bullying him towards ever more extreme attitudes. These two figures were preceded as mentors by another awful man, Jean-Jacques Rousseau, described by Diderot as 'deceitful, vain as Satan, ungrateful, cruel, hypocritical and full of malice', whose ideas, for all their apparent insistence on the natural goodness of man, are actually based on a deep distrust of human character and a loathing of civilisation and the modern world.

This raises a key question about Leo Tolstoy. Why did he yield so readily to three such malign influences, welcoming them into his life and cherishing them and their ideas for so many years? (Look again at Pierre Bezukhov, whose main sources of inspiration were optimists, a senior Freemason and a God-loving peasant.) Tolstoy's susceptibility cannot be a mistake; it has nothing to do with chance or stupidity. Almost literally, he fell in love with all of these men, keeping their portraits close by him. One or other of them loomed large with him from his mid-teens to the very end of his life. We shall have to look more deeply into this, but the explanation may be that he found in them what he had been searching for, external confirmation of his own dark view of the world and the people in it.

This is a huge story, barely containable as a 'brief life'. But even in outline, the experience and achievement of Leo Tolstoy is a fascinating account of overwhelming genius. The collision between the positive qualities and pessimistic doubts of this talented man produced a flash of energy bright enough to light up the world with two vast masterpieces of literature, and many other great works. It is this unparalleled achievement for which he is now remembered.

Childhood, Boyhood and Youth

One of the first significant incidents recorded in this man's early life is anything but Gargantuan; it concerns a modest item, a piece of wood that was both small and imaginary. When he was a little boy of five or six he and his brothers invented a remarkable game. They formed an imaginary community called the Ant Brotherhood, a simple and perfect society in which everyone loved everyone else and there was no conflict. The four of them would crawl into a little den of boxes and chairs, curtained by shawls, and cuddle together in the comforting darkness. The greatest secret of this cheerful fraternity was a little green stick on which the eldest brother, Nikolay, claimed to have inscribed a formula by which perfect happiness could be achieved and a Golden Age ushered in for all humanity. The lads spent many a happy hour pretending to look for the stick, which had been hidden in a small ravine on the estate of Yasnaya Polyana where they lived and played. Tolstoy is now buried, according to his wish, on that spot. The place where he lies is the geographical centre of European Russia, where the gloomy forest begins to merge into the southern wheat-lands.

As at most other houses in the early nineteenth century death paid regular visits to Yasnaya Polyana (Clearglade), the home and estate a hundred and thirty miles south of Moscow where Leo Nikolayevich Tolstoy was born and brought up. Death took away his mother when he was only two, his father when he was nine, the next year a devoted granny, and soon after that an aunt. But these domestic tragedies turned out not to be the disasters they might have been in another family. Parental care was still available in abundance. The family closed ranks, and other females, the grandmother and two aunts, took over the maternal role. As a result, in his earliest years little Leo was virtually swaddled in feminine attention. He was shown love in such abundance that the memory of it never deserted him, and he seems to have longed for the whole world to be turned into a place where that kind of affection prevailed over everything else. He and his siblings were brought up and educated in a kindly fashion, always cocooned by the warmest feelings of security. If ever there was a childhood of blessed happiness based on prosperity, enjoyment and love, this was surely it. The one drawback may have been that the children were raised in a highly moral atmosphere deriving its values from the Orthodox Church. Leo's inability to meet the moral standards set for him in childhood may explain much of his future self-dissatisfaction.

The boyhood that followed, which spent itself between Moscow and Yasnaya Polyana, was less than complete in its happiness. Young Leo was both unattractive and shy; much of his early adolescence was spent in self-regarding loneliness. The family moved to Kazan, where he entered the university at the (normal) age of sixteen, only for his brief undergraduate career to end in failure. He learned to carouse with his brothers and their friends. Adept only at bungling relationships with eligible young girls of quality, he was obliged to seek out young girls without quality to satisfy his physical needs – virginity had slipped away from him at the age of fourteen. He could smoke, drink and gamble as well as the next young man of substance. The bouts of dissipation would alternate with days of agonising self-analysis and raging conscience. Although he continually worked out plans and rules for living a good and useful life, these did not include diligence as a student. He left the university after less than two years because of 'bad health and domestic circumstances', and never regretted the abandonment of formalised education.

Failure was to remain a constant companion in his young life for some time to come. The age of twenty found him inheritor and master of the Yasnaya Polyana estate with its thousands of acres and hundreds of serfs. In a great surge of idealism he set about improving their circumstances in every way that he could think of, only for his grand plans to founder on the rocks of centuries-old peasant suspicion, stubbornness and stupidity. The role of gentleman farmer, which had so much appealed to him, soon ended in disillusionment that was hard to bear. And so to Moscow, and then to St Petersburg, for further rounds of debauchery and self-indulgence, now on a metropolitan scale and with gambling taking a huge toll on his finances. In neither city did he make a serious attempt to embark on a useful career. But he had long been a voracious reader, and now he began to write.

Years before, Tolstoy had formed the habit of keeping a diary, the hundreds of pages of which went beyond the recording of events, providing an opportunity for serious reflection. Other authorial tendencies included thoughtful essays which he set for himself (as opposed to any that might have been required by the university staff). 'Philosophical Notes on Rousseau', 'Concerning the Purpose of Philosophy' and similar texts lay on his desk, most of them half-finished, all of them indicating a serious turn of mind and an irresistible attraction to the trade of writing. His thoughts about religion were well advanced but inconclusive; several years earlier he had rejected the teachings of the Orthodox Church, yet he found paradoxically that a belief in God would not leave him. One way or another it never did.

Another contradiction in the human condition struck him time and again as intractable. At a young age he could think his way through entire philosophical systems and plan out on paper what was best for him and for the general human good. He convinced himself that his results were true and reliable. Yet he could not live up to them. 'It is easier to write ten volumes of philosophy,' he told his diary, 'than to put a single precept into practice.' (In his diary he had listed no fewer than forty-two Rules for Personal Development; the pages are full of anguish at his inability to follow them consistently.) Here were two of the major preoccupations that would haunt him for decades to come – the urgent need to excavate meaning and precept by hard intellectual effort (the little green stick principle), and recurrent disgust with his own human failings which not only kept him personally from moral stability but also, in the grand scheme of things, undermined any concept he might have had of goodness in the whole of humanity.

The story of the green stick speaks about the man himself. A desire for a world ruled by love and excluding violence, along with the wishful idea that complex human problems can be reduced by intellectual effort to a set of clear principles – these would remain the goals and values that lay behind a great writing career.

The logical outcome of such sensitivity, allied to a propensity for bookishness and note-taking, was an urge towards creative writing. It would be some time before Tolstoy produced anything that was all at the same time imaginative, fictional, artistic and complete, but in his early twenties he began to indulge in something that might be called 'semi-fiction'. Among several fragments that went beyond the diary and the essay was an attempt at a kind of autobiographical story, *A History of Yesterday*. Based rather obviously on the unstructured writings of Laurence Sterne, this piece rambles thoughtfully over many subjects – with more digression than narrative – and never, in fact, gets beyond the day before yesterday in the author's life. Some critics have seen in it an indication of the analytical power of Tolstoy's later genius; others prefer to point out its jejune emptiness and effortful straining at language. Either way, it confirms Tolstoy's unstoppable advance towards a writing career. These scattered notes on a laboratory bench were enough to convince the experimenter that he loved writing, and would soon know how to do it well. Scarcely more than a year later, in July 1852, he was able to send off to Nikolay Nekrasov, the editor of *The Contemporary*, a complete work about the length of this book, the first instalment of a planned four-part novel to be entitled *Four Ages of Development*. This section was called *Childhood*.

Tolstoy was off to a promising start. That long road that would end with his death as a worldwide celebrity at Astapovo railway station nearly sixty years later begins here, with the author's delight at the immediate publication of his first offering. Nekrasov deserves to be congratulated for his sensitive perception of the new writer's ability. *Childhood* is a slightly puzzling work best defined in negative terms. It is not a story with exposition, development and resolution. It is not fiction; neither is it biography, let alone autobiography. It is not about childhood itself, but about two sets of experiences on two days in a particular childhood, that of Nikolay Irtenev, one day in the country and one in the city. It is not a depiction of childhood in its essence or typicality, though the author pretends that it is.

Although there are clear instances of the volatility of a child's mind as he soars into ecstasy one moment and descends to despair the next, much emphasis is given to the charm, poetry and happiness of our young years. This is enjoyable, and makes for delightful reading, though it is surely an oversimplification. Tolstoy's own childhood was atypical in its special degree of privilege, security and enjoyment. Not many people would be likely to re-evoke this period of their lives without paying equal attention to vulnerability, fear, envy and the agony of waiting for the grown-up state to arrive since it is such an obvious improvement on being small and young.

There is a serious side to the work, though it is largely hidden, with the kind of subtlety that the same author would not always deploy in his later works. Nikolay, for all his tender years, is a thinker and a planner, analysing his way through his little life like the undeveloped great mind that he really is. Morality and conscience keep coming into the story. Whilst we cannot deny that in real life this kind of thing actually happened to Tolstoy when young, we have to conclude that these are not the most appealing passages in the story. It is not that they are improbable, simply that the older author's hand seems to obtrude at these points. Even the concept of mortality plays a significant role, with two deaths at the beginning and two more at the end, though this is not so heavy-handed as it may sound. There is no lingering on this deepest of all subjects; it is taken along naturally as indeed it had to be in real life at that time. This is a mere flickering of light that will one day intensify and focus itself unerringly on the problem of living with death. At this stage it is the innocent child who runs away from the adult and gets the prizes.

In formal terms, *Childhood* is a triumph, and it sets a method and a standard for the later works. The chapter units are short and neat, many of them beautifully constructed cameos or vignettes of character and incident. The style is an object lesson in clarity. For all of these reasons this early work deserved the approval of its first editor and several reviewers who took to it with immediate enthusiasm. It still gives delight to readers of all ages.

Despite their moments of quality, the subsequent *Boyhood* and *Youth* cannot match *Childhood* for energy and exuberance or for literary accomplishment. The two later sections are more diffuse and their narrative pace is slower. The stakes in Nikolay's young life are higher, and disappointments amount to something worse than embarrassment as he gradually declines from the ideal and undergoes an unavoidable process of corruption only too familiar to those who already inhabit the imperfect world of adulthood. So recently an enthusiastic child, he has become a brooding young person. There is a sense of modulation from major to minor as the younger years pass away. It is not that Nikolay himself descends into wicked behaviour, rather that he becomes aware of unfairness and cruelty in a world which has seemed until now to be based on joy and justice. There is no better example of this than his gathering awareness of how badly the world has treated his German tutor, Karl Ivanych, a man of warmth and noble character whom we know from the earlier work.

The Russian writer and critic Dmitri Merezhkovsky, an admirer of Tolstoy's frankness in describing his own life, has given us a succinct summary of his literary method which we shall do well to bear in mind throughout this story:

> The artistic work of Leo Tolstoy is at bottom nothing less than one tremendous diary, kept for fifty years, one endless, explicit confession. In the literatures of all times and peoples there will hardly be found a second example of an author who reveals his personal and private life, often in its most intimate aspects, with such open-hearted sincerity.

This 'diary' begins with these three semi-autobiographical sketches. Each is enjoyable in its own right, but taken together they also comprise an indispensable introduction 'to the life, career and works of one of the world's greatest writers of fiction, religion and moral theory.

A Monstrous Alter Ego

Tolstoy's reading at this time was wide, though unsystematic. In the course of it he came across the writer who would influence him more than any other throughout his life – the French thinker Jean-Jacques Rousseau (1712–78), whom he fell upon with mixed feelings of kinship and worship. As late as 1901, nearly sixty years after the event, he recalled that, 'At fifteen I wore round my neck, instead of a cross, a medallion with his picture.' In 1905 he wrote further, 'I am greatly indebted to Rousseau, and I love him.' This was more than admiration or sympathy; it was instant, enduring, ineradicable affinity. Tolstoy tells us that many of Rousseau's pages were so near to him that it seemed as if he had written them himself. 'Rousseau and the Gospels,' he told the world not long before he died, 'have been the two great and fruitful influences in my life.' This is not idle rhetoric. The ideas of the Frenchman have many parallels in Tolstoy's work, a few of them imitated, most of them instinctive. A search for truth, the elevation of primitive life over civilisation, the spontaneous love of nature, the rejection of class, wealth and property (in theory at least), disdain for the arts and sciences, the interest in educational theory and practice, an obsession with human corruptibility and especially the irrepressible problem of sexual passion, the branding of government as evil, the glorification of the emotions and the need to preserve the best aspects of religion

– all of this, and more common material, crops up time and again in the works of both writers.

At first sight all of this seems harmless enough: one great writer is instinctively attracted to another, and it shows. But what kind of a man has Tolstoy been drawn towards, and what lies behind the attraction? Rousseau the man is someone for whom no one has a good word to say. Denis Diderot was not the only man to call him a monster; Grimm and Voltaire did the same. In his book *Intellectuals*, the journalist and historian Paul Johnson tells us why:

> One modern academic lists Rousseau's shortcomings as follows: he was a 'masochist, exhibitionist, neurasthenic, hypochondriac, onanist, latent homosexual... incapable of normal or parental affection, incipient paranoiac, narcissistic introvert... filled with guilt feelings, pathologically timid, a kleptomaniac, infantilist, irritable and miserly'.

Add to this selfishness, humbug, dishonesty, meanness, self-pity, an offensive, querulous nature, total conviction of his own moral rectitude and a certainty that he was always right. Almost any defect of character you can think of seems to have belonged to this man, who set himself the goal of showing us what is wrong with the world, and how we should put it right.

Hypocrisy lies in the midst of it all. The man who preached friendship and love instantly estranged everyone he met. The man who had the interests of children at heart dispatched his five illegitimate babies to a foundling home from which very few children emerged alive. The man who proclaimed the need for truth was guilty of lying and distortion, not least in his ostensibly open-hearted *Confessions*. The scrupulous historian who wrote the famous work *Du Contrat Social* (*The Social Contract*) did so 'with a misleading air of dry precision and simplicity, which disguises the assumptions on which it is based and its disregard of the actual facts of history and the complexity of human affairs' (from the *Oxford Companion to French Literature*). We do not know how much Tolstoy knew about Rousseau's character and behaviour, but this is the man with whom he felt a lasting affinity, and it is clear that at least some of the defects outlined above existed in both writers. In any case it is not really the awfulness of Rousseau's conduct that concerns us here. The main point is this: what seems to have drawn Tolstoy to Rousseau most dramatically was his first reading of the *Confessions*. Henri Troyat tells us that they 'thundered through his brain like an earthquake'. The young Russian describes the moment of revelation: '"So, all people are the same as me," I thought with delight, "I am not the only monster born into the world with an abyss of sordid qualities."' This clue may lead us towards an explanation of Tolstoy's fundamental philosophy of life, seen here at a formative stage. Disgusted with himself and his own behaviour at an early age, unable to control his worst instincts, he could only assume there was something terribly wrong with him. Suddenly, he reads a text which tells him an awful truth: everyone else is just as bad as he is, probably worse. From this misanthropic assumption derives a dark impression of the world and its ways, one from which he will never recover, except during a few short periods irregularly punctuating his seven remaining decades. Rousseau has confirmed his worst misgivings about humanity, and, although others will endorse them, he will never see them unconfirmed.

At such an early stage in our story this may seem like an exaggeration. The sad thing is that the pattern of this meeting of minds with Rousseau will repeat itself twice in Tolstoy's life; there will be two further startling encounters with despicable men, with whom none of us would want to have any dealings, as men or as thinkers, because of their negative attitudes and their unreasonably misanthropic and pessimistic beliefs, linked to a certainty of their own righteousness. To have accepted a natural association with one negative alter ego like Rousseau might be passed off as a youthful aberration that got out of hand; to do this three times in a lifetime, ensuring that no period of it is free from the influence of such a man, suggests a need to preserve and keep renewing a deep-seated hatred of human life. If this is so, it is all the more remarkable that the same man wrote the best and most optimistic of all great novels, which we shall soon discuss.

Mountains and Warfare

In his late teens and early twenties Tolstoy had been casting around for something to hold his attention, but nothing did. Beyond bouts of youthful roistering and hunting, he dabbled in anything that came along – a little agriculture, a spot of law, a touch of music, some work for the local authority in Tula, a bit of translation (which took him well into Laurence Sterne), a snatch at passing ideas such as investing in a Hungarian company or joining the Ministry of Foreign Affairs. Then, at the age of twenty-two, he suffered a collapse of morale when his diet of wild oats began to lose its flavour, and it became clear that so far he had accomplished nothing and prepared himself for no kind of future.

The opportunity for a sharp change and meaningful occupation came when his brother Nikolay, who was due to return to military service in the Caucasus, offered to take Leo along with him. The younger man was astounded by the magnificent region of towering mountains, snowy peaks and hot springs to which he had been transferred. It had a savage beauty that caught his imagination and he wrote that he would sometimes spend hours on end contemplating a spectacular view. He observed the local denizens with the same microscopic intensity he had recently applied to the citizens of Moscow and St Petersburg, whom he had watched closely as they went about their business, trying to imagine the individuality of their lives.

This was not the gawping attention of a tourist, but rather a genuine interest and empathy working towards the habit and method of a novelist.

He also threw himself into soldiery with much enthusiasm, starting as a volunteer, then signing on and learning a new trade as a bombardier, which involved passing exams, and eventually putting his life at risk in sorties and skirmishes near the River Terek in a part of the world – the wooded ravines of Chechnya – that had seen off many young Russians already and would continue to do so down succeeding generations. His commitment was such that he was recommended for the award of a St George's Cross for bravery in action, though a bureaucratic delay prevented him from receiving it. His close knowledge of this geographical area and the actuality of warfare would serve him well in his writing, from early works such as *The Raid* (1853) and *Woodfelling* (1857), later tales like *The Cossacks* (1863), right through to *Hadji Murat*, the finest work of his last years, which was published only after his death. He still read voraciously during periods of inactivity, and he continued to say his prayers, keep his notebooks and think seriously about living a moral life, by eschewing sinful activities and doing as much good as he could, and also about planning for the future.

Tolstoy's stay in the Caucasus and experience in the army lasted a long time, two and a half years. Now, at the age of twenty-four, he was beginning to find his place in the world, and to know where his values lay. Morality and literature were the two forces quickening in his bloodstream; they would stay with him until the end. Meanwhile, he was still unable to live up to his own standards, and spent more time gambling and womanising than fighting the foe.

But there was another chapter of military experience waiting to be written. After only a few weeks of leave he was sent to join an artillery brigade in Bucharest, and then he volunteered for transfer to the Crimea, where Russia was resisting the first invader to set foot on Russian soil since Napoleon. Here he saw action on a scale that dwarfed anything he had witnessed with the hillsmen in the Caucasus. This was modern warfare with a vengeance, which involved large numbers of men living in inhuman conditions, suffering and dying in thousands – a bitter foretaste of the attritional warfare that would become infamous in the next century. And Tolstoy was in the thick of it. He was given charge of a battery of guns in the Fourth Bastion, the southernmost point in the Sevastopol earthworks, the most dangerous area in the whole theatre, barely a couple of hundred yards from the enemy and under constant fire. The only way to survive was to work flat out, sharing the perils, losses and triumphs with staunch comrades, joking with them and thinking of nothing but the good cause they were fighting for. This is the high point of Tolstoy's military involvement and patriotic spirit.

He worked in that hotspot for six weeks, and spent his free time writing. The direct result of this was the first of a series of sketches describing life in the front line. 'Sevastopol in December' was published the following June (1855), also in *The Contemporary*, and was read by the Tsar, who is said to have told the authorities to 'look after that young man'. By the time of publication Tolstoy's patriotic fervour had diminished, giving way to a certainty of the futility of war so deeply ingrained in his mind that it would never leave him. However, at that time his article, a passionate piece depicting the hardships and courage that were the everyday experience of Russian soldiers, which employed the strikingly unusual device of being written in the second person plural ('You choose the nearest one...'), had a positive effect on the whole nation, whose declining morale needed all the support it could muster. It was followed by 'Sevastopol in May' (also 1855), literally a different story, which ended with a now famous claim that its hero was nothing less than Truth, though that entailed an unvarnished depiction of inefficiency, corruption and futility far removed from the tone of the earlier piece. It was also a clear indication that that first sketch had been anything but the whole truth. The censor did not believe the public was quite ready for this degree of veracity, so he changed Tolstoy's bitterly critical piece into an item of government propaganda. The publisher had to issue the article, but he withheld the author's name. The third sketch, 'Sevastopol in August' (1856), was different again, a rather loose fictional account of two brothers serving at the front, in which Tolstoy's earlier passion, lyricism and didactic spirit were replaced by objective narrative interest.

This was an area of human experience in which Tolstoy had proved himself beyond doubt. He could easily have been killed, but he wasn't. Instead he was promoted to the rank of lieutenant for his bravery under fire, and by the time he got back to St Petersburg, still only twenty-seven years old, he was welcomed as a celebrity, known to everyone as a promising new writer, a successful if self-appointed war correspondent and an acknowledged hero. He retired from the army, and began to enjoy himself. On the cultural scene he soon got to know all the leading figures (except Dostoevsky, who was still away in exile – the two famous writers never met), Westernisers, Slavophiles, liberals, radicals, all of them. The novelist Ivan Turgenev arranged many of the introductions, and Nekrasov cultivated him assiduously, not wanting to lose this talented prospect to another publishing house. But in only a few weeks Tolstoy succeeded in alienating almost all of his new contacts. Always irascible and impulsive, he now adopted an attitude of such arrogance and truculence that no one enjoyed his company beyond a few close friends who went with him to visit restaurants, and to enjoy drinking and gambling sessions, and not a few gypsy girls. When Turgenev called him a 'troglodyte' he bestowed the term with amused affection, only to realise as the weeks went by that it was taxonomically exact. At this early stage Turgenev could just about tolerate Tolstoy's boorish behaviour, but their relationship was never going to prosper. It reached its lowest point in 1861, when there was such a furious row between them it almost gave rise to a duel. After that they severed all contact until Turgenev, on his deathbed in 1883, wrote a famous letter to Tolstoy, begging him not to abandon his art.

It was not long before everything turned sour. Conscience could not prevent him from misbehaving, but it invariably hurt him afterwards enough to spoil the fun. He loathed the social scene in St Petersburg, and nearly all the writers. There was nothing in the city to catch his imagination or hold his attention. His interests were simpler and clearer than ever before, and they would be best served in the depths of the country. Three ideas began to obsess him. First, he could no longer accept the system that kept him in wealth and idleness paid for by hundreds of serfs; immediate reform was needed. Second, he felt strongly that education was the key to improving the lot of the poor people, and he needed to know more about teaching methods. A third concept was still in his mind, though it would soon be shelved for a couple of decades: this was nothing less than the creation of a new religion based on a simplified form of Christianity purged of dogma and mysticism.

After taking advice on all sides, Tolstoy worked hard on a plan for freeing his serfs and providing them with land, but in the event they turned it down out of mistrust, and who can say they were wrong? The plan was generous, but its benefits would be a long time coming, and the landowner's interests were conveniently protected. The people gained their freedom any-way within five years, as did all the serfs in Russia, and this occurred without serious disturbances. Even so, the impending revolution that Tolstoy was predicting at this time now looks like something that was delayed rather than prevented.

His interest in the education of poor people could be made to fit with the one field of life-experience that remained to be explored as he came to full maturity: foreign travel. By going abroad he could complete his own education and study other people's methods of instruction.

Foreign Travel

Tolstoy made two trips abroad. The first lasted from early February until the end of July 1857. On the second occasion he left home in early July 1860 and was back home by the end of April 1861. Thus he spent a total of sixteen months away from Russia, and he never went abroad again in the half-century left to him. His grand tour, although taken rather later than was usual for the Russians and Englishmen who did that sort of thing at the time, had the desired 'finishing' effect: it gave him a broader vision of the world, confirmed most of his basic ideas and attitudes instead of overturning them, and left him with a clearer idea of what he was going to do, and not going to do.

Some of his adventures were landmarks in his life. For instance, when he attended an execution in Paris the experience affected him deeply. Having spent a couple of months enjoying all the city could offer in the way of entertainment (a great deal), he seems to have gone along to the guillotine that morning in the spirit of a tourist taking in another spectacle. But the sight of the murderer's head parting from its body, the thump as it fell into the basket, and the clinical deliberation with which the ceremony was conducted filled him with such horror that he left the city the very next day, and did so with his burgeoning views on anarchy confirmed. With an enormous leap of false logic he decided that if a state could carry out an atrocity like this, all government must be wrong. 'I shall never serve *any* government anywhere,' he wrote to a friend, and he never did. But the suddenness and extremity of this commitment, inspired by however distasteful an event, tells us much about the temperament of this great writer. How could an intelligent young man make a mistake of this magnitude, and live with it for the rest of his life?

Another significant event occurred when Tolstoy travelled from Lucerne to Baden-Baden. His plan was to proceed from there to Holland, London, Paris again, Rome and Naples, and perhaps go back home via Constantinople. Alas, none of this came about, for one simple reason. He went to try his hand at the notorious roulette wheels of that town, lost a little, risked and lost a lot more, borrowed, lost again, and ended up thousands of roubles down and with no money to survive on, let alone gad about the western world. It was Ivan Turgenev who (among others) bailed him out, and the whole ghastly incident would repeat itself only a year or two later in the same town, with Tolstoy replaced by Dostoevsky, who also lost thousands and was helped out by Turgenev. Both of Russia's greatest novelists suffered from uncontrollable gambling mania and lost vast amounts of money, though there was a difference between them. Dostoevsky's agony at losing was the greater, because Tolstoy had richer friends and a good deal more equity to fall back on. As a young man he had gambled in St Petersburg and in Moscow; as a soldier he had gambled in Chechnya and in the Crimea. He lost at cards, at the roulette table and even at Chinese Billiards (whatever that may be). In 1862 he managed to lose yet another thousand roubles in Moscow. He lost money always and everywhere, despite the advantage of knowing he had an infallible system that was just about to recoup his losses. It is clear, however, that neither of these great writers was interested in money as such. What they wanted was intense excitement. They felt truly alive when beset by risk and hazard, wild contingency, and this feeling was more attractive and habit-forming than any physical drug. Uncertainty and unpredictability guaranteed passion and pleasure in their purest form.

Today, if you visit Yasnaya Polyana, you are likely to be shown a non-existent room twenty feet up among the beech trees. That is what Tolstoy used to point to when people asked him where he was born. Unfortunately, the actual house is no longer there. It was sold off and taken away, stone by stone, to pay off one of Leo's bigger gambling debts. He moved into the large wooden house that stands nearby, now a famous literary museum, the place where *War and Peace* was written. Gambling mania blighted Tolstoy's life for at least a decade and a half; this and sexual desire were the two impulses over which he frequently lost all control. He never wrote an entire work on the subject (unlike Dostoevsky, whose story, 'The Gambler' (1866), was dictated to a stenographer in twenty-six days), but you will find a harrowing description of a young man trapped by a card-sharp and losing tens of thousands in *War and Peace* (Volume Two, Part One, Chapters 13–16). Both writers eventually overcame this obsession by settling down with a beloved woman who turned out to be a good organiser and a strong personality. Before that happened to Tolstoy, his experience as a gambler is likely to have nurtured in him a fascination for randomness and indeterminacy that would underpin the theory of history shortly to be outlined in *War and Peace*.

Meanwhile, having cut short his first trip abroad, he found he had been virtually forgotten in the big cities at home. Perhaps people were more interested in the impending emancipation legislation; perhaps he had made himself even more unpopular than he had thought. Either way, his name was not on everyone's lips. But his time away had not been wasted. Even while travelling he had steadily added to his literary output, and by 1860 he had quite a string of publications, including 'Notes of a Billiard-marker' (1855), 'The Snowstorm', 'Two Hussars' and 'A Landowner's Morning' (all 1856), 'Lucerne' (1857), 'Albert' (1858), 'Three Deaths' and 'Family Happiness' (1859).

He now spent many months back on his estate, trying with varying degrees of success to get to grips with farming and estate management. His second trip abroad was more properly concentrated on education and prison reform; he paid a number of visits to schools in several countries, and talked pedagogy whenever the opportunity arose. In London he asked a group of Chelsea schoolboys to write about what they had done that day. These little essays were taken back to Russia where they are preserved in the Tolstoy museum, neatly written pieces in traditional copperplate, now rather faded, but clearly legible and full of amusing detail. Tolstoy learned a lot from his researches, and confirmed his leaning towards German educationalists like Auerbach and Friedrich Froebel, who believed that a child's mind should be left to develop naturally and spontaneously rather than being force-fed by rote learning.

One other important event occurred during this second trip abroad. His brother Nikolay, ill with consumption, had been advised to go abroad, and his doctors sent him down to Hyères in southern France. Leo went along too. Within a month Nikolay was dead, having expired in his younger brother's arms. His moving demise is painfully recorded in fictional terms, in *Anna Karenina* (Part Five, Chapters 16–20, the last of which is the only chapter in any of Tolstoy's long works to bear a title – 'Death').

The Teacher

Tolstoy's interest in teaching went back a long way. His first attempt to create a school and teach the peasants how to read and write had begun in 1849, and at first he had every reason to think his project was going well, though in fact it was doomed. Not only was the whole enterprise illegal, as he found out later, but it was staffed and run by inexperienced people, and in any case it collapsed before long because there was no money to employ anyone or buy in materials – Tolstoy's debts had caught up with him, and had to be paid off.

His desire to teach was sincere and well founded. First, he was fond of children and they responded to him, so he was at his happiest when entertaining young people, playing with them or teaching – and these things often went on at the same time. Second, he knew instinctively that existing methods of education were boring, cruel and stultifying. And third, he was shocked to discover how widespread illiteracy was. He knew about his own peasants, but had vaguely assumed things were better elsewhere. Alas, during his military career he had discovered that there was hardly a soldier who could read or write. Between his two periods of active service, in Bucharest, he had drawn up a plan for the elementary education of servicemen, but this came to grief when he was posted to the Crimea.

It was on his return from abroad that he entered the most serious of his periods of teaching. He set up a school, ran it well, attracted large numbers of pupils, who were taught free of charge, developed original ideas for the curriculum and new teaching methods, took part himself in most of the classes, wrote dedicated materials for the classroom including a primer and a book of suitable stories, and edited a periodical in which he described his theories and methods, which ran to twelve issues. His work culminated in an impressive essay with a title that indicates part of his policy, 'Who Learns from Whom, the Peasant Children from Us or We from the Peasant Children?'

Tolstoy's ideas would eventually catch on, and some of them entered the educational system employed all over his country, though they have not survived, or at least not flourished, in the modern age. The reason for this is that, as in many other aspects of Tolstoy's thinking, he goes to extremes and wanders a long way away from real life and common sense. Something akin to his approach was last employed several decades ago in the United Kingdom under the name of 'progressive education', a process that was child-centred, ill-disciplined, disorganised and intellectually undemanding. Some primary schools were divided up into small group areas where, if a child felt like it, he or she could wander in and ask to be taught how to add up, draw or read a book. The shortcomings of the experiment soon made themselves obvious, and the principles behind it have been largely abandoned, much to the impoverishment of children today, whose education has returned (fortunately without the cruel punishments) to a regimented, over-organised, narrowly prescribed and continually examined system not far from the one that Tolstoy was so keen to supplant.

Tolstoy's basic idea was that children should not be coerced into schooling, but that education should be made so interesting that they would prefer to have it rather than do nothing. They should be shown how to love learning. With this in mind there should be no enforced curriculum, no rewards and certainly no punishments. No bells, no timetable, no rules, no testing. The young people would be required only to show what they were interested in by asking questions, which would be answered and followed up along any lines that developed. Tolstoy got his numbers up to forty (including a few girls), and eventually as high as seventy. It was discovered that the pupils responded best, and could be taught to read with the least difficulty, between the ages of six and eight. By the year 1862, the high point of his experiment, there were thirteen working schools in his locality, and they enjoyed such a good reputation that some of the richer peasants sent their boys in from twenty or thirty miles away. The children were prepared to put in a long day, sometimes of twelve hours or more. There was a good deal of play, but they also read stories from the Old Testament and a series of folktales and legends which he rewrote himself for their consumption. Aylmer Maude, Tolstoy's best-known English friend, translator and editor, claims that these versions 'have reached more readers, and perhaps benefited the world more, than anything else he wrote'. This may have been an exaggeration at the time it was written, and it certainly is now, but it gives an indication of the serious achievement of this famous writer in an area little known to the general public. He would continue to write fables and simple didactic stories throughout his career. During the period 1859–62 he wrote little else.

Where did it all go wrong? Eventually Tolstoy seems to have run out of steam in the classroom and decided to concentrate on communicating his ideas in theory rather than in practice – hence his educational periodical. When working as his own village-schoolmaster he had been able to inspire a small team of like-minded young assistants, and all of them had toiled willingly, teaching with warmth and enthusiasm over many long hours, days and weeks, relaxing only during the summer when the boys were needed to work on the land. It is significant that as soon as the master withdrew his labour there was no one among his disciples capable of taking the scheme forward into permanent establishment. Tolstoy's powerful leadership, unstinting hard work and inspirational energy had been crucial to the whole enterprise, and without him it could not go on.

The great qualities and serious defects of this remarkable man – his originality, self-certainty, altruism, expressiveness, love of language and literature, his all-round intellectual strength, ranged against his naivety, remoteness from reality, lack of common sense and flexibility, along with incorrigible extremism, and with doggedness thrown in on both sides of the equation – are nowhere better characterised than in his career as a pedagogue.

But now he was ready to move on into the happiest, most successful and most significant period of his life, without which no one would still be reading his fables and educational theory.

Family Happiness

Each of the few short decades given to us has its own character, but perhaps the most rewarding is the run of years that takes us from thirty to forty. It is a time of hard work, but for those who have used their twenties to establish a personality and a likely career, and to settle themselves in emotional terms, this period of early maturity brings huge satisfaction, from willingly accepted responsibilities, growing confidence, family happiness, endlessly renewable vigour and a continuing sense of immortality. So it was for Leo Tolstoy. He could look back on years of uncertainty, and, if he had known it, look forward to decades of worry and disillusionment (mainly spiritual) on a massive scale, but for a few years in the 1860s he knew the exciting happiness of a fully formed man growing through to personal fulfilment, creativity and nothing less than greatness in his chosen field of literature.

First, he got married, in September 1862. His attractive young wife was not easily acquired, and not immediately satisfied, or satisfying, when she was his. To begin with, even when he settled on a suitable household with interesting girls (the Bers family), there were three of them: Liza, statuesque, beautiful if rather cold; Sofya (known affectionately as Sonya), sentimental, rosy-cheeked, dark-eyed and melancholic; and little Tanya, with her shining black eyes, puppy-like vivacity and many talents. Tanya was a little too young; instead of choosing her as a partner he put her lovingly to one side, waiting to revitalise her as Natasha in *War and Peace*, who has been described as 'the most wonderfully made character in any novel' – rather more than she ever became in her unhappy real-life marriage to a dull cousin. (A rival claim is put in, incidentally, by George Meredith, who called not her but Anna Karenina 'the most perfectly depicted female character in all fiction'.)

Liza was the obvious choice, first in line for marriage at the age of nineteen, pushed forward by her father and eagerly awaiting his proposal. But no. He flouted both convention and paternal opposition by choosing the second girl. It was the best decision he ever took. Sofya turned out to be the most wonderfully made literary spouse. If he is one of the great men of world culture, she is the traditional feminine force behind him. There is no secret about this, but the magnitude of her role and influence has perhaps not been fully acknowledged.

Sofya was eighteen when Leo proposed, scarcely into full womanhood, overwhelmed by this big, mature man (he was thirty-four), star-struck by his literary fame (she knew his works by heart) and unashamedly impressed by his aristocratic title (she could see herself as a countess). But he knew quality when he saw it. His young wife took little time to prove herself as an ideal companion, attractive, strong in physique, intelligence and personality, a hard worker and capable organiser. She was also gratifyingly fertile, giving birth to their first child nine months and five days after the wedding, and going on to produce another twelve children at the rate of one every two years until as late as 1888, when she was in her mid-forties and he was sixty.

The love between them was at first genuine and overwhelming, though its intensity would not be matched by durability. It was tested at the outset when, before their marriage, the mature writer who had spent as many years as she had been alive building up manly experience in a man's world, thrust his diaries into her hands and insisted she read them. This name-day present was intended as a gesture of openness, the clearing away of impurities before their new life together could begin, but as an ingénue she was unprepared for its frankness. The author's indiscretions were all there, including his sexual adventures, all of them squalid, right down to the protracted liaison with a peasant woman on his estate that had been broken off only a few weeks before, having produced his bastard child. She never forgot or quite forgave the shock of disgust and horror delivered by this sudden introduction to male depravity.

Nonetheless Sofya got through it all somehow, and soon they were settled at Yasnaya Polyana. Letters, diaries and other people's memoirs all testify to a period of unforgettable honey-moon happiness, though it wasn't long before the inevitable decline set in. It was then, before she was twenty years old, that Sofya discovered maturity and strength almost overnight, sufficient to show that she was a match for the titan she had linked herself to.

Within a matter of months she had begun to take charge of things. When the bickering started she gave as good as she got. And in most things it was her will that prevailed. First, she had to feminise the rough old house, starting with soft pillows and going on to carpets and curtains. Then she began to delineate responsibilities: she would manage the household (which she did with astonishing efficiency for such a young person) while her husband ran the farming side of things (much less effectively).

It was obvious that she was equal to her husband in most things and much better than he in some that mattered. This had one salutary effect of huge significance. She was able to organ-ise, control and galvanise this man in such a way that he was able to make a start immediately on what would turn out to be his great masterpiece. In some respects, at the beginning of 1863, she was the facilitator of *War and Peace* as much as she was the mother-to-be of his first child. But her innate ability and strength of character held a corresponding disadvantage. If he was moody and unpredictable, she could surpass him in the depth of her disappointments and the ferocity of her emotional outbursts. What this would lead to eventually is almost too painful to behold, even at a distance of thousands of miles and five or six generations: for all their early love and mutual dependence, this marriage turned out to be one of the most turbulent, antagonistic and hateful in cultural history.

Who was to blame? In response to this question opposing forces line up as at the battle of Borodino, with massed ranks and much ammunition. The latter consists of a multiplicity of notes, diaries, records, memoirs and observations – there is a huge amount to go at. The pair of them even kept rival diaries in their later years in order to do each other down and wrench the transcript of their ill feelings and arguments back into their own direction. There is little point in apportioning blame. Leo Tolstoy was cruel in his selfishness, but his depressions, regrets, inconsistencies, self-questioning, agonies of conscience, sudden decisions and uncontrollable bad temper were matched by her anger, resentment, malevolence and hysteria, which grew over years into paranoia. One cardinal point separates them in all of this. Sofya Andreyevna did not set herself up as a beacon for mankind to follow, did not preach to humanity about how it should live and die, did not set impossibly high moral standards that no one (least of all the setter of them) could ever live up to. She did not announce to the world that God is love, and the secret of human happiness lies in tolerance, forgiveness, charity and Christian humility. Her husband, sooner or later, did all of these things.

Meanwhile, though, in the early 1860s, the first years of their relationship and her early twenties, they worked together closely and their successes were many. Sofya produced their first baby, and went on to produce more, which brought them huge happiness along with the unremitting hard work and worry that parenthood involves. That was fine for them; what matters more for us is the way in which the world's greatest novel emerged from their relationship at this time.

Before *War and Peace*

First, however, it will be useful to glance briefly back over Tolstoy's literary career so far. At the age of thirty-five, he was now an established writer with half a million words behind him. It was time to publish his first *Collected Works*, which came out in 1863 in four volumes, and these excluded a number of drafts that would be published later. This is a promising assortment; a good number of these works would have been remembered if the writer's career had gone no further, but they vary in quality as much as in subject matter.

Among the longer works of this period was, for instance, *Family Happiness* (1859), Tolstoy's first attempt at a conventional novel, which is well told but weighed down by his unrealistic ideas about women. It is told in the first person by Marya Alexandrovna, who marries an older man, whom she loves at first though she soon cools towards him, and is drawn away by the attractions of society life. After almost being seduced by a handsome Italian she returns in remorse to her husband, and they settle down again, to enjoy a more mature form of love based on family life. The idea of a woman having to tame her wild sexuality and replace it by dull, safe domesticity is one that will return in later works, but in this novella the didactic spirit predominates, and it is too obvious that Tolstoy is less interested in telling a good story than in responding to George Sand's ideas about female emancipation and free love that were all the rage in St Petersburg.

Shortly before that Tolstoy had written 'Two Hussars' (1859), in which the philandering of a father in a provincial town is followed up twenty-odd years later by his son, who returns and meets the same people, though he doesn't quite manage a similar seduction. The irony is that no one was shocked by the father's licentious behaviour because of his dashing personality and generous spirit, whereas the son, a product of a later era of scientific rationalism, is what one critic calls 'a calculating materialistic prig'. He seduces no one, but leaves behind a worse impression than that left by his immoral parent. This tale is out of line with anything written by Tolstoy at this time. It is an unusual story with a strange twist, which deserves better than the relative obscurity in which it now rests.

In the same year, 1859, Tolstoy wrote 'Three Deaths', the first of several fictional works with dying and death as their main subject. Despite some convincing dialogue and portraiture, covering numerous characters from all social classes, this turns out to be another didactic piece, with a silly idea at its centre. The suggestion is that in order to die well you need to have lived with as little education, sophistication and prosperity as possible. A rich old lady dies in agony, a simple peasant manages his death without difficulty, and a tree expires in complete indifference. Half an hour's pleasurable reading cannot hide the fact that Tolstoy is following Rousseau too closely by magnifying the advantage of living close to nature and away from the corrupting effects of civilised living.

At the beginning of 1863 we can detect a strong sense of this writer clearing the decks for action. Much tidying of old drafts went on, from which three important, and very different, works emerged. *The Cossacks*, which had been gestating in notebooks and diaries for more than a decade, tells the story of Dmitri Olenin, a restless and introspective young man, disillusioned by the modern world, who decides to throw it all up and go back to nature *à la* Rousseau. For a while he discovers a kind of happiness in a new, outdoor life among the Caucasian Cossacks, but he is eventually rejected by them. In the figure of Yeroshka, an old Cossack veteran, Tolstoy has found a model of Rousseau's natural man, who exists only for himself, follows his own feelings, and goes about with confidence, living through God in nature. But Olenin finally has to acknowledge that, because of his education and civilised upbringing, he has forfeited any possibility of achieving such an existence for himself. Worst of all, he has found that the ordinary impulse of falling in love with a woman (who is there, but unavailable) has destroyed his will to give up selfish gratification and live for others. Happiness is not to be found in self-sacrifice. This story has been deeply admired by serious critical minds from Turgenev onwards; there are those who consider it his masterpiece before the great novels. Others may find its narrative purpose diffuse, and its assault on civilised values excessive and simplistic.

An entertaining and moving tale of this period (not published until 1885) was *Strider*, which is both original and full of extended meanings. It is the tale of a horse, mostly told by the horse, a piebald gelding, who knows what it is to be an outsider, having been rejected even by his mother. His perceptions of human behaviour come as something of a shock to us; he cannot understand our ideas of nobility and private property. But most of the story is about his horsey qualities, his varied life, decline and death – he was based on a real animal with a huge stride and a fine turn of speed. Ivan Turgenev was so impressed with the authenticity of this effort that he believed Tolstoy must have been a horse in a previous incarnation.

One of Tolstoy's most accomplished and disturbing novellas is *Polikushka*, written earlier but published in 1863, without attracting much attention. Polikushka is a peasant horse-doctor with a dreadful record as a petty criminal, who reforms himself and is rewarded by the mistress of the estate when she excuses him from military service. (At that time conscription was a terrible fate for a young man, who would go away for years on end and perhaps never return.) But then he loses a large sum of money entrusted to him, and the result is catastrophic. The story tightens its grip as we worry increasingly about Polikushka's temptations and misadventures, while also agonising over how the village conscription problem can be solved – who will go in his place? The stakes are high, the characters, mainly peasants, are among Tolstoy's most memorable portraits, and the undeserved but inevitable outcome puts us through more than one grievous twist of suffering. This is a good example of Tolstoy allowing the story and characters to dissolve his urgent message in sheer narrative interest, though it is never lost sight of. The uselessness of violence, the cruelty of war, the need for forgiveness and love, the hypnotic power of money – Tolstoy has built up a powerful case on these ideas, and no reader could leave this tale behind without taking them away with him.

One disturbing real-life event that occurred in 1866 is worth lingering over if only because it troubled Tolstoy and lay on his conscience for the rest of his life. Two officers from a regiment stationed not far from Yasnaya Polyana came to him one day and asked if he would act as defence counsel at the court martial of a clerk, Vasiliy Shibunin, who, when drunk and provoked, had struck his Commanding Officer. This was one of the few offences for which the death penalty was automatically applied to a guilty verdict. Tolstoy accepted the assignment and worked at it assiduously, writing out a long speech in which his argument depended on a plea of temporary insanity. Although he felt he had done all he could, the wretched man was found guilty and shot in a field not too far away, in the manner of the horrific executions witnessed by Pierre Bezukhov towards the end of *War and Peace* (Four, One, II). Tolstoy never felt he had let Shibunin down, but he did live to regret mounting a defence on legal grounds rather than falling back on the moral law and the law of God. This dreadful incident must have gone a long way towards confirming his horror of the death penalty and his impatience with government and judgment of any kind. Our knowledge of this shocking occurrence makes his later intransigence in these areas, particularly in his last novel, *Resurrection*, rather more understandable.

Returning to literature, we can see that this writer's experience and imagination have been expanding story by story. All it needs now is for the many positive qualities of his literary output to be drawn together and used to animate some larger enterprise. We can sense the rising tide of a major work in the occasional diary entry written down only a few months into the happy period of early marriage. 'Someone has advised me in all sincerity that it is wrong for me not to use my time writing. It's a long time since I remember having such a strong urge... to write... The epic manner looks like the natural one for me.' These jottings are the first hint that at some profound level Tolstoy knew he was about to undertake a work of monumental size and significance.

War and Peace

We know a good deal about the origins of *War and Peace,* and it is clear that the novel grew in the seed-bed of the husband-and-wife relationship. In personal terms, Sofya gave him support, encouragement and organisation just when they were needed. Beyond that, the novel was full of her family as well as his. This is not surprising; one critic reminds us that 'Almost every particle of *War and Peace* bears a relation to something in Tolstoy's personal experience.' Two-thirds of this novel are scenes of peace rather than war, and for them the author plundered real life in search of interesting characters and relationships.

Tolstoy was very fond of the family into which he had married, and spent much time with these good people. As well as several characters, some famous scenes in the novel derive directly from their experiences. Tanya Bers, Sofya's younger sister, provides some of the best examples. When Natasha persuades Boris to kiss her instead of her doll Mimi, this is a faithful copy of what Tanya did to her future husband. More striking is Tolstoy's use of this young girl's experience at her first ball, which took place at Tula in the presence of the heir to the throne. Young and inexperienced, she felt lost in the socialite maelstrom and certain to be ignored, but her loneliness and despondency soon turned into triumph and happiness. Beyond that, an elopement episode between Natasha and Anatole Kuragin is based on a real event: Tanya's real-life would-be seducer was himself called Anatole. Tanya and Sofya's elder sister, Liza, bears a strong resemblance to Vera, Natasha's elder sister. Boris Drubetskoy is formed from two people close to the Bers family. And so on.

The main characters of the novel, however, come from Tolstoy's own family. The Bolkonskys and the Rostovs have prototypes in several members of his dynasty who were alive and active during the period in which the novel is set, 1805–12. His maternal grandfather, Nikolay Volkonsky, has developed into Andrey's fierce father, Nikolay Bolkonsky. His daughter, Marya, derives from the real-life Marya Volkonskaya, Tolstoy's own mother. And so on. Scholars have gone into the closest detail, much of it provided by many discarded drafts which Sofya scrupulously collected and conserved. The overall conclusion is worth having, if not too surprising: the much-vaunted authenticity of Tolstoy's characters is underpinned by personal experience. In this novel there are five hundred of them. As the Russian critic Nikolay Strakhov pointed out, 'Even the dogs have names.' And the horses.

The novel began life as the story of a man exiled after the abortive uprising in 1825 by a group (mainly army officers) known as the Decembrists. This coup went off prematurely and was cruelly put down, with the ringleaders hanged and many participants sent to Siberia, from where they began to return two decades later. Tolstoy's first idea was to tell the retrospective story of one of these rebels. But the more reading he did, the further back he went into his country's recent history, and he became fixated on Napoleon's invasion of Russia in 1812, and then the preceding years. So he then planned a work called *1805*, which began to be published serially in 1865. (A draft variant called *All's Well that Ends Well* was rapidly discarded in 1866, and immediately transcended, but that has not stopped it being reconstituted by scholars and published as a spurious 'Original Version' of *War and Peace* or, worse still, published in English in 2007. The thought that anyone might buy this watered-down version of the novel is not easy to live with.) In March 1867 Tolstoy hit on the final title, and, although details kept changing, and the number of volumes rose from four to five, then six, the final novel was under way, and it was finished in 1869, by which time Sofya had given birth to their fourth child.

The best of all the early editions, the one that should be used now as canonical (though there is still some dispute about this), is the one approved by Tolstoy in 1873. Two major changes were introduced into what had been offered before. First, a number of long passages written in French in the earliest editions were changed into Russian, Tolstoy having realised he could indicate when characters were speaking French rather than bother the reader with bilingualism. (This has become more important in our time since in those days a good knowledge of French could be taken for granted in an educated readership, which is not the case now.) Second, he combed his novel out into something more straightforward by removing many passages of philosophical and historical argumentation, which had rather weighed down the text hitherto. These were not discarded, because they had their own intrinsic value, but they were scraped together into a single section which now supplies the second epilogue. Contrary to popular belief, no more than half a dozen short chapters (out of 366) indulge in any kind of serious lateral speculation, and they occupy important strategic positions, such as the beginning of a new volume or section. And yet, the myth persists among people who have not read it that the whole novel is bogged down by unnecessary speculation.

Another persistent misconception maintains that *War and Peace* is, as described by Henry James, a 'large, loose, baggy monster'. It is nothing of the kind. The novel has been scrupulously arranged into a series of tiny units which are then assembled into larger sections, and these are thematically coherent and distinctive. He used the simple formula that had stood him in good stead and would do so again and again. Its basic unit is a very short chapter. For those who want to remain convinced that this novel is formidably difficult it may come as a surprise, but the chapters of *War and Peace* average out at *four pages long* (about fifteen hundred words), and only one or two chapters in the whole work run as far as ten or eleven. This is a useful device in his shorter works – it runs through them all from *Childhood* to *Hadji Murat* – but in the big novels it is invaluable. The reader never feels lost or in any danger of being swamped. A possible break in the reading is never more than five or ten minutes away. Gradually the little units build into a solid section, then the scene changes, another section forms itself and after three or four of them a whole volume is at an end. In this way, 366 easily managed chapters arrange themselves in seventeen sections, which are presented in four separate volumes. About one-third of the subject matter is war, and, while the shadow of warfare is never far away, a good two-thirds are devoted to peaceful activities.

A similar point can be made about the innumerable characters. The large total of them may sound formidable, but once again the grouping of massive material is its saving grace. Our interest soon focuses on three families: the Rostovs, the Bolkonskys and the Bezukhovs. Count and Countess Rostov have formed a family rather to Tolstoy's liking (and not unlike that of the Bers). It knows how to live well and look after its own (especially in adversity, of which there is a lot), displaying much affection, mutual support and a spirit of generosity that the old count has taken to extremes, steadily ruining them financially. In the younger generation the two important people are brother and sister: Nikolay and Natasha. Count Nikolay Bolkonsky is a severe old widower-patriarch who has brought up two children under rigid discipline. Marya is cowed by him, showing defiance only in choosing religion as a personal refuge. Her brother Andrey, wishing to follow a military career like his father, admires Napoleon and thirsts for personal glory. The young Pierre Bezukhov, although a bastard son, inherits his father's title and huge riches without the slightest idea of what to do with them.

The central ground of the novel is taken up by Nikolay, Natasha, Pierre and Andrey as they progress from youthful uncertainties and yearnings to a hard-won maturity and understanding. Between them, they cover all the problems, disappointments, triumphs and disasters that make the lives of all of us so rewarding and yet so difficult. Perhaps this is the essential theme and true originality of *War and Peace*; the people who find life to be a struggle are not the poor, neglected and downtrodden who figure so prominently in many another nineteenth-century novel, but youngsters born into privilege and wealth. It is not poverty or deprivation that makes life hard; it is life itself, which, as the Russian proverb has it, is not just a walk across a field.

Natasha is Tolstoy's greatest single success. He depicts her entire development from childhood to maturity, motherhood and domestic happiness, and her bumpy career involves her in every conceivable feeling from ecstasy to despair as it takes in love, engagement, separation, boredom, attempted elopement, humiliation, a suicide attempt, deep depression, reconciliation, compassionate nursing care and the death of a loved one before she emerges into new love leading to marriage and the creation of her own family. Everything about her is described with skill, sympathy and a close knowledge of femininity (which must have come partly from Sofya, though her husband's expertise in this area didn't do her much domestic good). She represents a wholesome, instinctive approach to life that Tolstoy believes comes naturally to women and never to men.

The two male protagonists derive from the author, dividing him down the middle. Andrey is mind, intellect, calculation. Pierre is emotion, soul, spirit. Their careers alternate throughout the book – a pleasing narrative device – since when one is enjoying a rare period of relative success and enjoyment the other is down in his fortunes, and vice versa. Pierre is the richest man in Russia and marries the sexiest woman on the social scene. Andrey, also very wealthy, is married already to a pretty princess and his first child is on the way. Who could lose out with advantages like these to begin with? These two men can, and do, on a personal scale that matches in microcosm the disasters that fall simultaneously on their beloved country as it is overrun by the French army. Between them they confront every hardship and danger you can think of: blazingly unhappy marriage, animosity, love and loss, duelling, sickness, spiritual disillusionment, peril on the battlefield, wounding and pain, acute depression leading almost to despair, arrest, imprisonment, real and mock execution, and repeated disappointment in every direction taken in search of consolation and guidance. In one case, early death. Their two lives are anything but a walk across a field.

There is one splendid moment in the novel when the fourth figure, Nikolay, finds himself *running* across a field. Having fallen from his horse in an early skirmish, and badly sprained his wrist, he expects to be helped when he sees men running towards him. Alas, they are French soldiers and he only just survives by running away from them. As he does so he is all but whimpering at the injustice of it all. 'Who are these men? They can't want to kill me. *Me*. Everybody loves me!' The cosseted boy of only a few years before has been wrenched forward in time out of his nursery into an alien world of violence and aggression. The shock of surprise delivered by a first taste of reality has been sensitively captured by the writer. Nikolay represents the virtue of pragmatism – with his youthful indiscretions behind him he is well served by hard work, application and down-to-earth realism. Unintellectual, unspiritual, altogether untheoretical, he eventually achieves greater success, fulfilment and happiness than either of the two main protagonists.

Between these fictional characters and the real historical personages – Napoleon, Kutuzov and a hatful of generals and diplomats – there is a small universe that swarms with living people. They are portrayed with every last touch of realism, which gives them greater authenticity than the big historical figures, most of whom are at least slightly distorted by satire. This is not accidental. Tolstoy has a thesis to advance. He wants to puncture the posturing of the top people in history, and those historians who pander to them with sympathetic interpretations of their role and effectiveness.

As to the ordinary people in *War and Peace*, let one example stand for many. Yefim, the coachman, comes into the story only once (Volume Three, Part Three, Chapter 17). With the wagons all loaded and ready to move off, he refuses to get excited:

Old Yefim sat perched on his box, not bothering to look round. Thirty years of experience had taught him it would be some time yet before he would hear the magic words, 'Off we go, and God go with us!' and even when they were uttered he would be stopped again at least twice to send back for something that had been forgotten, after which he would still have to pull up one last time for the countess herself to stick her head out of the window and beg him for heaven's sake to take care going downhill. Knowing all this he waited philosophically, more patiently than his horses, especially the near one, Falcon, who wouldn't stop pawing the ground and champing the bit. At long last they were all on board, the steps were folded away, doors slammed, a forgotten travelling-case was sent for, and there was the countess with her head out of the window saying what was expected of her. Only then did Yefim remove his hat with a deliberate gesture and make the sign of the cross.

'Off we go, and God go with us!' said Yefim, putting his hat back on. 'Pull, me beauties!'

Yefim, this chance acquaintance, irrelevant but endearing, with his mature humour and wisdom, is welcome to his brief flourish on the stage of literary history. In a large novel there is enough time and space for him. It is the likes of him that enliven, extend and humanise the whole story; people like him pop in and out of the narrative in the way that we run across people in real life who happen to be there though they are not going to play any further part in our lives.

Tolstoy on History

Nothing in *War and Peace* has been as controversial, and mis-represented, as the author's observations on the workings of history. The case is confidently put by Isaiah Berlin, who warns us that the historical and philosophical passages have been looked on:

> … as so much perverse interruption of the narrative, as a regrettable liability to irrelevant digression characteristic of this great, but excessively opinionated, writer, a lop-sided, homemade metaphysic of small or no intrinsic interest, deeply inartistic and thoroughly foreign to the purpose and structure of the work of art as a whole.

But they are simply not like that.

In the first place, most of them were removed by the author from the main text of the novel, and collected together in Part Two of the epilogue. It is now quite wrong to describe the novel as weighed down with this kind of speculation – though this does not stop the myth being recirculated by people who would like to have read the novel but have not bothered to do so. The truth is simple: these ideas do not clutter the novel.

But the most surprising discovery for anyone who reads the Second Epilogue is that the passages are not difficult to read, not tedious, not lopsided, not unoriginal, not uninteresting.

They are new, forward-looking and fascinating. They have two purposes. The first is to castigate and revile Napoleon, cutting this 'military genius' down to the size of a microbe. The second is to castigate and revile the historians who have told his story and accepted the myth of his genius.

Who shall say Tolstoy is wrong on the first count? Napoleon, who now lies in glory at Les Invalides, is still revered as one of the greatest heroes of military history. His legend lives on – that of the man who united France, defeated nearly everyone in war and would have brought peace to the whole of Europe had he not been unnecessarily obstructed. This is a one-sided view of the man. He can also be seen as a cruel and petty despot who ruined his country and reduced it in size; the conqueror in Africa and at Austerlitz was also the abysmal failure at Trafalgar, Waterloo, in Spain, and worse still in Russia. The overall mission that he failed in was an attempt to force his will on a continent by ruthless militarism and tyrannical control. Tolstoy, seeing him in this light, undercuts this titan by depicting him satirically as a pompous little man with a blubbery body and podgy little fingers, who knows and cares nothing about the great country and people he is overrunning. He then mercilessly exposes the great man's unbelievably expensive blunders in strategy and tactics. As a portrait it is bitterly amusing to behold, but you are left with the impression that Tolstoy's biased view stands nearer to the truth than any of the grand tributes bestowed on the self-proclaimed Emperor by friendly historians. Tolstoy has every right to ask questions about a military genius who managed to reduce nearly half a million men, 150,000 horses and a thousand guns to almost nothing in less than nine months in Russia before deserting the few soldiers that survived.

Tolstoy goes further than this, however. He wants to show us that the very process of studying and writing history has always been fundamentally flawed. Take pitched battles, for instance. The accepted description of them allows for a wise and well-informed figure taking stock and controlling things from above the battleground by issuing clever orders which are followed directly and lead to success. But this is not how things happen, not ever. Here are two interchangeable passages that tell the true story of warfare:

> People forget the extent to which commanders-in-chief are constrained by circumstances. The circumstances encountered by a commander-in-chief in the field bear no resemblance to any we may dream up at home in a cosy study. The general is never in a position to contemplate the full significance of what is taking place… the commander-in-chief finds himself in the very midst of a most complex interplay of intrigue and worry… constantly called upon to respond to an endless flow of suggestions, all contradictory.

> Never, never, never believe any war will be smooth and easy, or that anyone who embarks on the strange voyage can measure the tides and hurricanes he will encounter. The Statesman who yields to war fever must realise that, once the signal is given, he is no longer the master of policy but the slave of unforeseeable and uncontrollable events. Antiquated war offices, weak, incompetent or arrogant commanders, untrustworthy allies, hostile neutrals, malignant fortune, ugly surprises, awful miscalculations – all take their seat at the Council Board on the morrow of a declaration of war.

The first is by Tolstoy, slightly abbreviated from Part Two of the epilogue to *War and Peace*. The second, which makes exactly the same point, was written by Winston Churchill in *My Early Years*. Corroboration by a mind of that quality suggests that the idiosyncratic Russian needs to be taken seriously.

Where the historians get things all wrong, he tells us, is in their simplistic, mechanical, reductionist idea of how events unfold. Cause and effect are not what they seem to be. The forces at work in human history are beyond logic and reason, and no outcome stems exclusively from what looks like its proximate cause. Nothing is certain. Every occurrence is contingent, one tiny thing after another ramifying outwards towards infinity. The forces that matter in history, on the battlefield, in society and in all human lives are chance, randomness, multivalence, probability. Indeterminacy is lord of the universe.

Almost nobody understood this line of thinking, any more than the reading public could understand Dostoevsky's Underground Man, who was making the same point at the same time (1864) and shocking everyone by the absurdity of his idea that $2 \times 2 = 5$ is as valid as (and more valuable, more useful, more real and more human than) the sloppy notion that only $2 \times 2 = 4$ has validity. It is astonishing that two different independent minds, both more literary than scientific, should have hit on this enlightened insight independently and at precisely the same time, in the same country and culture. In rejecting popular modern materialist thinking, which looked so plausible in its algorithmic complacency, these two writers were anticipating the enormous scientific changes of the twentieth century, in which the commonsensical 'truths' of Euclid and Newton were to be shattered by Einstein, Heisenberg, and all their successors. Nowadays you cannot move in the world of science without taking account of the uncertainty principle, chaos theory, fuzzy thinking, fractal geometry, probability theory and well-established ideas about the sub-atomic world that seem so crazy they make Tolstoy's and Dostoevsky's once-shocking assertions seem like modest little intellectual propositions. Their challenging proposal that the universe is not describable in simple terms – *by common sense and reason alone* – has been validated many times over.

Despite some repetitiveness, Tolstoy's thoughtful epilogue is full of striking ideas, often backed up by colourful metaphors from everyday life. It is a remarkably good read, and should on no account be neglected. There is evidence that some people do read it and understand. Peter Riddell of London's *The Times* recently referred to a political crisis by describing it as 'a Tolstoyan world of unpredictability and uncertainty'. This is what Tolstoy should be remembered for; it brings out the originality and relevance of his greatest novel, which lie behind the enjoyable stories and characters that are immediately accessible and fully acknowledged.

There is one final quality enjoyed by this novel that puts it in a class of its own. It is radiant with optimism. Despite the innumerable difficulties, disappointments, bad decisions, pain and cruelty, tragedies and deaths suffered by so many of the characters, most readers, like Orlando Figes, will easily identify it as 'a triumphant affirmation of life'. There are simply too many moments of joy, experienced by too many characters, for the spirit of tragedy to prevail, or even last for long. Natasha's girlish triumph at her first ball, her father dancing the Daniel Cooper or entertaining a famous general, soldiers getting themselves noticed by an emperor, the radiant goodness of Platon Karatayev in captivity, children playing, adolescents falling in love – events like these cram the pages of the novel, reminding us how good it is to be living. Anyone who needs to restore strained tissues should reread the whole of Volume Two, Part Four, when an entire family enjoys itself over a long period, playing together, hunting, celebrating with good food and drink, singing and dancing, riding in troikas under the stars, visiting good neighbours, telling fortunes, falling in love. The setting is Russian; the feelings are universal. Martin Amis captures this rare quality in a single question: 'Who else but Tolstoy has made happiness really swing on the page?'

One word of warning. Not only is this great work an island of optimism in world literature, it is exceptional in the works of this master. Elsewhere in his work you will not find the same sustained and reliable *joie de vivre*, not even in *Anna Karenina*.

Poison in the Soil

By the end of 1869 the first edition of *War and Peace* had sold out, and the author was basking in national acclaim. Sofya was happy with the role she had been playing and the royalties were rolling in (though Leo would soon regard such earnings as immoral). Not all of the comments on the novel had been favourable. For every conservative critic ready to castigate Tolstoy for questioning the patriotism of the Russian nobility there was a radical only too keen to object to the novel as backward-looking and biased against *him*. Nobody wanted to accept, and few could understand, his apparently anarchic view of Russian history. In any case, he needed a rest not only from controversy, but from writing itself.

He plunged into a period of intense activity, which involved two new preoccupations: reading widely and learning Greek. No half measures with that language. He bashed through it in three obsessive months (1870–1), during which he said he lived in Athens from morning to night and spoke Greek in his sleep. Soon he could read Xenophon and was moving on to Homer and Plato. A Classics professor tested his claim to full knowledge of the language by reading unprepared texts with him, and had to pronounce the examinee competent.

Tolstoy had not lost his interest in teaching young people how and what to read. In the autumn of 1871 he returned to a plan that had been waiting for development, an *ABC* with the subtitle:

First Book for Reading and a Primer for Families and Schools, with Directions for Teachers. He worked at this task with utter devotion, telling people he had put more work and love into this book than anything else he had done. He reworked folk tales, legends and stories from history into shortened versions written with great simplicity and clarity. He also added some of his own stories, and they are among the best. In later life, when he had rejected most of his earlier work, he felt able to claim *A Prisoner in the Caucasus* and *God sees the Truth, but Waits* as the finest things he had ever written.

Before long he would be writing his second major novel, and although *Anna Karenina* is regarded by most people as a great treasure, and by some as his masterpiece, it is surely a lesser achievement for being narrower in scope and darker in tone than *War and Peace*. Its first word is 'Vengeance' and its last significant event is bloody suicide, which had been inexorably predetermined. The current of Tolstoy's former optimism has drained away, or, to be more precise, the optimistic aspect of this second novel is occluded by unpleasantness and ineluctable tragedy in the main story. For some reason, a balance in the mind of the author has been tipped against sweetness and light. In *War and Peace* Tolstoy has dealt directly with the unpleasantness of human existence, but still managed to assert its ultimate goodness. Now we see a mirror image of that proposal – that there are some good things about living a human life, but they seem not to preponderate. The point is put succinctly by Theodore Redpath: '*Anna Karenina*, despite many passages and even whole chapters abounding in *joie de vivre* and humour, is shot with a sense of disillusion, and at times clouded with pessimism.'

What could have happened to this great writer for him to move noticeably from marginal positive to noticeable negative on an issue as important as this? Usually, it is not possible to identify a culprit in such a situation, but this time a villain can be identified. He is an unpleasant influence, a man who has diminished human happiness and made a strong contribution to the uncertain, pointless, godless world of suffering that has been foisted upon us increasingly in spiritual terms over the last six generations. We have seen how Tolstoy's life was affected by the 'monstrous' Rousseau; now the malign presence of a second awful person darkened his days, just at the time when disappointment with marital bliss was setting in (the summer of 1869), and it changed him forever.

We are speaking of Arthur Schopenhauer (1788–1860), a man thoroughly disliked by his own mother at both ends of his life; she couldn't stand 'his gloomy outlook' in childhood, and she never once spoke to him for the last twenty-four years of her life. *Chambers Biographical Dictionary* describes him in the following terms: 'Throughout his unhappy life he was dark, distrustful, misogynistic and truculent... His work is often characterised as a systematic philosophical pessimism.' Another one says, 'Schopenhauer's philosophy is stunningly and famously pessimistic. His work is certainly not the right sort of thing to read on a beach.' If you look up 'Pessimism' in any companion to philosophy you will find this man dominating the article; hardly any other philosopher will merit a mention. The *Oxford English Dictionary*, without claiming that he invented that term, uses his name to define it. Schopenhauer believed in the total wretchedness of the world we live in, and the nastiness of human nature. For him life is something that ought not to be, and this is the worst of all possible worlds. David Berman tells us that, 'For Schopenhauer the world is so bad that if it were to become even slightly worse it would collapse into chaos.' Most of us would not want to go near such a man, or listen to his ideas, yet Leo Tolstoy welcomed him into his life. Schopenhauer's portrait was placed on his study wall alongside that of Charles Dickens. At the end of this work we shall have to bring Rousseau and Schopenhauer together, add a third name to this roll of dishonour, and consider why Tolstoy felt immediately and lastingly attracted to three such shockingly unpleasant mentors, who one after another accompanied him throughout his life's journey to its end. The answer will provide more shadow than sunshine.

Some aspects of the German's thinking did little harm to his new disciple. It has been claimed that Tolstoy's ideas on history, sexuality and art derive partly from Schopenhauer, and that this can be seen as early as the epilogue to *War and Peace*. This may be so, but the direct and baleful influence of this thinker on Tolstoy's philosophy, although noted in passing by all biographers, does not seem to have been given its full value, even though it can be demonstrated in the clearest terms. Only one commentator has put the charge directly: Redpath is bold enough to say, 'I strongly suspect that Schopenhauer helped to precipitate Tolstoy's next breakdown.' He is absolutely right. The truth of this stands out clearly when you look at the evidence. On 30th August 1869 Tolstoy wrote a long letter to his friend Fet (who introduced him to this thinker, having been under the German philosopher's influence for at least five years before that), exclaiming that all summer he had been 'in an ecstasy' over Schopenhauer's works, all of which he had acquired and read closely. *Only four days later*, Tolstoy suffered one of the worst experiences of his whole life, and this must have derived directly from his absorption with the dark German. For the record, Schopenhauer, described by Tolstoy as 'the greatest genius among men', will intervene in his life on at least two more important occasions, as we shall see.

The trouble started just as Tolstoy finished *War and Peace*. Now, in his full maturity, at the zenith of his physical and intellectual powers, bursting with vitality and nurtured by success, he should have been a happy man. But on the contrary, the sheer goodness of living seems to have made him all the more obsessed with the inevitability of death. What he had, could be taken away, *would* be taken away, soon. His wife described how he felt at this time: 'Often he said his brain hurt, some painful process was going on inside it, everything was over for him, it was time for him to die.' Much of the pain must have come from his immersion in Schopenhauer, whose poisonous pessimism was enough to make a happy man sad, and a sad man suicidal. (The German even wrote a treatise in support of suicide, though for some reason he failed to put its logic into practice, and lived on to over seventy.) Immediately after writing to Fet, Tolstoy set off for the distant province of Penza in the hope of buying some land, and broke his journey in the small town of Arzamas. During a sleepless night he was suddenly seized with dread. He described the feeling as follows:

It was two o'clock in the morning. I was exhausted. I wanted to go to sleep, and I felt perfectly well. But suddenly I was overwhelmed by despair, fear and terror, the like of which I have never experienced before... such an agonising feeling... God preserve anyone else from experiencing it.

Eleven years later he recalled the occasion in an unfinished work of fiction, *Notes of a Madman*:

I had hoped to get rid of the thing that was tormenting me in the room. But it came out behind me and everything turned black. I became more and more frightened. 'This is ridiculous,' I told myself, 'What am I afraid of?'
    'Me,' answered Death. 'I am here.'

Tolstoy's spiritual agony at this time cannot be overstated. He never fully recovered from this shocking encounter with mortality. His dark thoughts on suffering, death and the meaninglessness of life itself stayed with him, and were reflected in much of his subsequent work, particularly the last sections of *Anna Karenina* (1875–7) and the whole of *A Confession* (1879–81). In the early months of 1870 (more than a year after Arzamas) his mental and physical health broke down to such an extent that he said, 'Never have I experienced such misery. I do not wish to live.' He was in the grip of what we would now call a mid-life crisis, but, since this was a man who never did things by halves, it was of titanic proportions.

The multiple irony in the distressing circumstances of 1869 is striking. First: within a few months of completing the world's most life-affirming novel he becomes obsessed with dying and death. Second: Schopenhauer's philosophy is so black that it sees life as nothing but suffering, a constant striving without any satisfaction; death, then, should be warmly anticipated as a welcome release. Yet the knowledge of death, far from providing a soothing promise of relief, ruins what small happiness can be found in living. Third: although Tolstoy couldn't have known it, at the time when he was addressed so ominously by the voice of death, his life was actually at its meridian. He had lived for forty-one years, and had another forty-one still ahead of him. At that time, incidentally, the expectation of life in Russia stood at forty-one years.

It was in this newly poisoned soil that the seeds of his next big novel were planted. This accounts for the difference in tone to which we have referred.

Anna Karenina

This novel enjoys a reputation almost equal to that of its distinguished predecessor. Not a few people prefer it. The heroine is one of the most famous portraits in world literature. Her tragic misadventures and the web of marital and amorous relationships that constitute the main storyline of the novel are so convincing that one English columnist has recently recommended a good read through *Anna Karenina* as more beneficial to those in need than any conceivable course of marriage counselling.

On the face of it, the early stages of writing this novel took the same course as *War and Peace*. The author struggled over a long period with his first source material, which was to be historical – formerly it had been the Decembrist movement, now it was the time of Peter the Great. This was abandoned, false starts were made and there was much chopping and changing until the proper work began, only for it to lapse into an accumulation of outlines, notes and drafts that would differ a great deal from the eventual novel. All of this happened with both novels. But there was one difference, and it is crucial. Whereas *War and Peace*, once under way, developed organically into something unanticipated by the author (including various possible conclusions), *Anna Karenina* had its ending determined at an early stage: the heroine was going to commit suicide. The famous epigraph, 'Vengeance is mine, and I shall repay,' was in at the beginning. (By the way, this seems to have been borrowed from Schopenhauer's *'Mein ist die Rache'* – 'Mine is the vengeance'.) Even the ambiguity of these biblical phrases, indicating either the inevitability of adultery leading to punishment or else the need for us to leave it to God to arrange such things, leaves no doubt that Tolstoy had decided Anna's end even as he began. She was doomed to destruction, and the certainty of this, confirmed repeatedly by omens, hints and symbols, overshadows the novel as it proceeds. The story marches towards its predestined conclusion with the inevitability of a Shakespeare sonnet proceeding to its final couplet.

Anna herself came to Tolstoy in two stages, abstract and concrete. His very first idea (1870) was to write about a high-society woman guilty of adultery. The problem would be to make her sympathetic despite her culpability. The story goes that, after a long period of deliberation and replanning, he was suddenly inspired to get going by reading a simple line from Pushkin. Too much has been made of this. Pushkin's conciseness has nothing to do with Tolstoy's expansive manner of writing. If anything this is an attraction of opposites; he must have been hypnotised by a sudden awareness of the expressive potential of his native language itself rather than Pushkin's particular use of it. (The single word *s''ezzhalis'*, for instance, contains or implies so much information about people driving out of town and gathering together that it would take several English words to provide a decent translation.) In any case, the real impulse for writing came not from a literary source but from a recent event in real life.

Some months before, Tolstoy had been involved in a grisly incident. A neighbour of his, Bibikov, had a mistress, Anna Pirogova, who ran away from him in a fit of jealousy. Three days later she returned to the district, went to the local railway station and threw herself under a train, having sent an accusatory suicide note to Bibikov. Tolstoy saw the mangled body under post-mortem examination, attended the inquest and never forgot the experience. It would soon be transposed into one of the most famous events in world literature, which has been much discussed. D.H. Lawrence saw Anna's suicide as an act of self-mutilation on Tolstoy's part, the result of the author's piled up guilt, and a thirst for vengeance against a woman who personified one of the things he most dreaded – sexual passion. There is something in this, but it does make Anna sound more like an object lesson than an interesting character. Other critics have usually been kinder to Tolstoy, claiming that Anna's suicide is the logical outcome of her temperament and conduct, the natural product of unusual psychology worked upon by social ostracism. Thus Tolstoy's moral purpose is undeniable, but it is achieved with such subtlety that readers do not feel they are being manipulated.

In fact, Anna's character, situation and behaviour were meticulously planned and executed by the author. We have an unusual insight into this process of artistic creativity through the notes and early variants (at least seventeen of them) which have come down to us, carefully preserved once again by Tolstoy's wife. The most obvious changes were in the physical appearance and temperament of Anna and Alexey Karenin. They were turned into their opposites. Karenin began as a pleasant, if rather shy man, not bad-looking; Anna was coarse, vulgar and physically unattractive. In the finished novel, however, we shall see many references to Anna's charismatic beauty, not least when she meets Dmitri Levin in Part Seven, Chapters 9–10. Conversely Karenin has been turned into a desiccated bureaucrat with an icy manner and annoying physical mannerisms (such as cracking his finger-joints). Somehow Tolstoy catches a delicate new balance which allows us to see and understand why the wife deserts the husband; she is repelled by him, as we are ourselves. Besides which, he is now twenty years older than his wife. So when she meets a handsome young officer who is his opposite, Vronsky (another Alexey), she is ready for a fall, which happens not just naturally but inevitably.

Not that this is the single heinous sin for which Tolstoy condemns her; it is only the beginning of her immorality. Her wrongness consists in putting self before duty, and particularly in abandoning her son, Seryozha, and destroying the family that she has created. The most obvious preoccupation of this novel is with marriage, the family and their attendant problems: monogamy and sexual freedom, adultery, forgiveness, divorce, and all the social and psychological things that go wrong when the ground rules are infringed. A clear indication of this is given in the famous opening sentence of the novel: 'All happy families are similar; every unhappy family is unhappy in its own special way.' This silly epigram, which contains some wit but no truth or wisdom, at least gives an indication of what the novel is going to be about.

The story has a marvellous beginning, much superior to the rather tedious soirée at the start of *War and Peace*. Anna's brother, Stiva, wakes up from a bad dream in a strange place, on the couch in his study, and remembers something awful. He is in dire trouble, having been found out by his wife, Dolly, in an affair with their children's governess, and not for the first time. On this occasion, she has had enough, and his family life is in ruins. By the end of Chapter 4 we know everything about these people and their children, and have been treated to an exquisitely painful row between man and wife, which has a bizarre ending, with Stiva unable to do or say the right things and ending up with an asinine grin on his face, the agony of which stays with him more acutely than anything else. No reader can be indifferent to this; we have been drawn instantly into a situation which we need to know more about. How did it all happen, and how will things work out?

Help is on the way. Stiva's sister, Anna, has been called in to mediate. An eventual destroyer of human relationships is summoned to advise on the saving of a marriage. (You would have to be a re-reader of the novel to catch the full comic irony of this, but plenty of readers do return for more.) Soon we shall know about Anna's unhappy marriage, and watch it unravel. Somehow, Stiva's marriage survives this trial, like all the others, and our sympathies are with both of the contestants. Dolly is nothing less than noble in her capacity to forgive, and Stiva is just Stiva. How we can tolerate his awful behaviour is difficult to understand, but he belongs to a category of people well understood by the author. (The Rostov family in *War and Peace* provide other examples, especially in the old Count.) These persons know their own faults, but don't see themselves as villains. They mean well, and the one thing they have going for them is a rare and captivating quality that enriches the lives of everyone they encounter and overrides their obvious deficiencies. This is something difficult to define but instantly recognisable – a kind of effortless, mesmeric charm. A recent American president exudes this attribute, and the measure of its effectiveness is that it is not even necessary to name him. He and Stiva are birds of a feather. In both cases the erring offender uses all his redoubtable charm to persuade us that sexual dalliance isn't quite as wrong as it may seem because it was undertaken for fun and enjoyment, which makes it unthreatening at the deepest level. Anna Karenina, on the other hand, gave in to something Tolstoy regarded as thoroughly wicked – animal passion, which puts everything and everyone at severe risk. Selfish pleasure can just about be condoned; bestial physicality is of a different order of blame, a reversion to something much more dangerous.

These two marriages have to be matched against a third one, which closely parallels Tolstoy's own. It is that between Kitty (Shcherbatsky) and Konstantin Levin, the latter being a thinly veiled reincarnation of Tolstoy himself (*Lev* Tolstoy). In a brilliant piece of counterpointed plotting his adventures and development are set against the more sensational love affair between Anna and Vronsky, and its terrible aftermath. The two storylines wind around each other like the spiralling coils of DNA, to the enrichment and benefit of both. To take a single example of the contrast between them, Anna's ecstasies and misfortunes take place in an urban setting, whereas Levin bumbles along in the countryside. The sense of alternation repeats a technique thoroughly mastered in *War and Peace* and widely used in this novel, inviting further comparisons, between metropolitan and provincial life, Petersburg and Moscow, Russia and Europe.

Without Levin the story of Anna would be a gripping narrative with a strong moral purpose; with him on board the novel takes on a seriousness and significance that raise it to a new altitude. What began as a fictional work about a sinning, sexy woman ends up as an autobiographical work about an author from central Russia. Has anyone truly noticed either the cleverness or the full extent of Tolstoy's skilful manoeuvre? This famous work is called *Anna Karenina*. The heroine is among the most famous in world literature. She is largely responsible for the enormous success of the narrative. What has not been fully revealed is that the Levin-Tolstoy character, instead of providing a distracting foil or subplot, dominates the novel and takes up most of its space. Anna appears in sixty-eight chapters, Levin in a hundred. Some sub-plot. Even Kitty, surely a minor character within the main group, almost equals Vronsky in numbers of appearances (about fifty chapters each).

This is surprising, but it is not the disaster it might have been. In the first place, as we have seen, all of Tolstoy's fictional work is autobiographical, some of it minutely so, and this accounts for its authenticity. That quality lends itself to a whole string of events taken straight from the author's life: Levin's mother died when he was a baby, he keeps fit through gymnastics, bungles reforms on his estate, proposes via a lover's code, forces sexually explicit diaries onto his new bride, sits with his brother until his death, goes out haymaking with the peasants. Let no mistake be made: interesting things happened to the author in real life, and they are turned into fascinating fictional stories. (See, for example, Levin's panic over the birth of his first child (Seven, 14).) Most important of all, Levin declines into doubt and despair towards the end of the novel, and his spiritual agonies raise the tone of the whole work, forcing even the most casual reader to think about life, death and the meaning of it all, just what the Russian novel is (in)famous for insisting upon.

As to the marriage between Kitty and Levin, it is meant to be shown as exemplary, as was the one between Pierre and Natasha. Tolstoy's views on marriage and the role of women (as distinct from the family) are not enlightened, and now seem outdated. (This stands in contrast to his advanced ideas on education, from which we could learn a good deal today.) Tolstoy loves women, and there is hardly an author who has written about them more perceptively. The trouble is that he is desperately afraid of women while they are sexually available, and he sees them as a great danger. The power of an attractive woman was something he knew about from agonising personal experience, and he wrote a number of works on this subject to point out the dangers of uncontrolled sexuality. (See especially *The Kreutzer Sonata*, which we shall discuss below.) Accordingly he wants to see women married off, desexualised and kept permanently busy with running a household and raising children. If they thicken out bodily, take no pride in their personal appearance and lose their physical allure, so much the better. Kitty virtually disappears from the novel once she has had her first baby, so we do not see her reduced to this state. It is better represented by Dolly, who, although only thirty-three years old, is safely disposed of as a sexual threat because she is the mother of five living and two dead children, faded, plain and unremarkable, and the condition gains its fullest expression in the motherly figure of Natasha at the very end of *War and Peace* (First Epilogue).

What matters more, however, is Tolstoy's view of the family unit, which is worth serious consideration. He sees the family as something that is natural to our species, important and so valuable it must not be threatened by unfamilial behaviour. The people in this novel who lack a solid and happy family background themselves become poor homemakers. Neither Karenin, Vronsky nor Anna has that advantage, and Stiva suffers from the deficiency so badly he is virtually undomesticable. The Shcherbatsky sisters, Dolly and Kitty, by contrast, have emerged from a close, loving family and turn out to be staunch and devoted wives and mothers when their time comes. Anna Karenina's worst offence is to have destroyed such an institution. Tolstoy's message is clear: life must be based on solid, permanent relationships, which cannot be created, let alone sustained, by sexual passion.

The tragedy of Anna and Vronsky, although complicated by other factors, is that they were incapable of replacing the permanent, if imperfect, structure that they demolished by one of even equal durability (despite having a child of their own) because sexual excitement is not enough to sustain happiness and withstand adversity. Which is precisely what good families can do, as we know already from the Rostovs in Tolstoy's earlier novel. Here, at least, Tolstoy is on more solid ground. Six generations later, with the world a very different place, it is clear that his useful warning has gone unheeded. At least some of our modern ills, especially those of young people, derive from a collective reluctance to place a high value on keeping families together, which has been accompanied by increasing self-interest, immediate gratification, and greater irresponsibility in human relations. To this extent *Anna Karenina* remains a lesson for our times.

All of this makes the novel sound dreadfully didactic, which it is not. Moral prescriptions are not handed down from on high with a heavy hand; they are implied by the natural if dangerous development of events, and shaded over with enough ambiguity to make us wonder where we stand as one bad decision leads to another. Anna does wrong, but even as she does so she soon reaps a rich harvest of sympathy in the reader when she finds herself brutally ostracised by social snobs who themselves condone infidelity, especially in young men or as long as it is discreetly hidden. (Even today a promiscuous young man can be seen as a 'stud', whereas his female counterpart can count as a 'slut'.) Before that we have been struck by her open-hearted honesty, which stands in marked contrast to Karenin's concern for form and the niceties. 'I am a bad, wicked woman,' she thinks to herself, 'but I hate lying and pretence. He can't live without them... He is saturated with falsehood... He's not a man, a human being, he's a puppet. He's not a man, he's a ministerial machine.' His very name sounds square in Russian, and in English (one of the few tiny advantages of translation) cranial, therefore cerebral. And sure enough, this is confirmed when, despite taking the news of Anna's adultery with an outward show of near-equanimity, he is truly rattled by Anna's hysterical behaviour at the races, because of the impropriety involved. His reaction to her admission of infidelity is, 'I must insist on the preservation of appearances.' He seems more worried about losing his reputation than his wife. Tolstoy has achieved one of his strongest successes in building up this woman into a figure that we can understand and identify with. Despite his prejudice against her he has put a lot of goodness into this character, and it goes down with her, leaving a lot of other people's unacknowledged wickedness behind. As one critic puts it, referring to the 'subtlety and sympathy' of Tolstoy's judgements, 'the novel recognises no black or white, but only the infinite gradations that come between them.' This generosity of spirit is what turns her ultimately into a tragic heroine rather than a pathetic spectacle or a pasteboard picture of morality.

The construction of the novel is convenient and pleasing. Once again, we have a succession of unformidable tiny chapters building into substantial sections. (The average length of a chapter is just over three and a half pages.)These are arranged not quite geometrically, but with agreeable regularity, three fairly long ones, one short; the same pattern repeats itself: aaabaaab. The longer sections contain between thirty-one and thirty-five chapters; the shorter ones nineteen and twenty-three.

The subject shifts interestingly between Levin/Kitty and Anna/Vronsky; there is rarely a run of more than eight or nine chapters in any one camp. This is controlled and facilitating; there is no danger of tedium or disorientation. It simply makes a long novel easy to get through. That Henry James considered Tolstoy's organised writing to be large, loose and baggy (though he probably read his version in a loose French translation) testifies only to the superficiality of his reading.

There are two technical matters in *Anna Karenina* that have created controversy, and have not been settled. They will never be, because nothing about them can be proven; individual preference will have to sit in judgement. First, the novel is replete with omens, dreams and symbols, in a way that *War and Peace* was not. Some critics believe they are obvious and overdone; certainly they are unsubtle. (Although a lover of good poetry, Tolstoy lacked the lightness of touch ever to write any himself.) For example, a fatal accident at the rail terminal in Chapter 18 occurs immediately after Anna and Vronsky have met for the first time, a clear prefigurement of their tragic destiny, and even the death of the heroine. Another famous symbolic occurrence is at the races in Part Two, Chapters 24–25, when Frou-Frou, a thoroughbred mare of some style and beauty, is mishandled by her rider, Vronsky, and comes to grief, having to be put down after breaking her back in a fall. The parallels between Vronsky/Frou-Frou and Vronsky/Anna are too obvious to need spelling out. At first sight these devices, dragged out into open view, look clumsy, even obtrusive. But other critics have not been worried by them. In the first example, the death of the watchman, which comes very early on, before the leading characters have even established themselves, is reported rather than described, and, brutal though it is, the incident takes up only a few lines. As to the death of Frou-Frou, we can hardly disagree with the critic (T.G.S. Cain) who points out that the race itself is a 'convincingly, indeed excitingly real steeplechase, involving the real death of a living and not an allegorical horse'. No one is compelled to stop and calculate the correspondences. On the whole, this subject is perhaps less important than it seems. The average reader may not even notice the rather heavy-handed symbolism that has worried professional critics, though they make a living by spotting such things. Indelicate though Tolstoy's touch may be, this is not enough to bring down his novel, nor even detract from its powerful effect.

Disagreement also attends the last section of the novel, which is really an epilogue, though it is not named as such. Anna is dead, and the story is over, but you still have nineteen chapters to get through. The first four or five clear away a few necessary details, then we are left with Levin/Tolstoy for another forty-odd pages. In one sense this can all be dispensed with. It is almost always omitted, for instance, in stage, film or radio versions of the novel, on the obvious grounds that in narrative terms this material is anti-climactic; when you are presenting *Anna Karenina* as a good story, it will be diluted by any philosophical ramblings of the author tacked on at the end. Conversely, it is Levin who raises this work from the level of entertainment to serious literature capable of making the reader think and perhaps even improve his or her way of living. In these last chapters Levin undergoes a dreadful spiritual crisis, descending almost to suicide before the terrible, unanswerable questions of the human condition.

Levin's problem is that he has been infected with the same nasty bacillus that brought his author to the brink of despair and suicide at Arzamas in 1869 – Arthur Schopenhauer. In the ninth chapter of the last part Levin goes back to his books in search of any philosophical reassurance to be discovered in the great thinkers. He mentions Plato, Spinoza, Kant, Schelling, Hegel and Schopenhauer, but the last-named is the only one that he draws out for individual study and further emphasis. Schopenhauer's big idea was that the will to live makes human suffering inevitable, and death is the only release from it. Fascinated by the idea, Levin tries to adapt the German's system by ludicrously substituting 'love' for 'will'. This fails catastrophically. First, to do that is not only to falsify his subject, it is to arrive at its polar opposite. And in the second place, the relief provided by this betrayal of Schopenhauer's truth lasted only a day or two. The dark pessimist was too strong to accept either amendment or refutation.

Somehow Levin struggles through, helped by the example of a man called Platon, who lived by love and for God. (This is the second time Plato has come to the author's rescue; Platon Karatáyev had had a similar effect on Pierre in *War and Peace*.) This idea uncomfortably displaces Schopenhauer, and gives Levin something to live by, on which note the novel comes to an end. But Levin's thinking at this time of crisis seems to confirm that we have not exaggerated the malign influence of this single philosopher on Tolstoy himself. Schopenhauer has thrust himself forward again, causing a second spiritual crisis. For final confirmation, we shall see how he returns once more in Tolstoy's *Confession*, which lies just around the corner.

Anna Karenina is an enjoyable and important novel, one of the world's indispensable literary treasures, but the tightening intensity of its main story and the firm grip of inevitable tragedy prevail over the good nature of Konstantin Levin by such a wide margin (even though he has the last word) that it is surely outclassed by the broader human experience of *War and Peace*, a work that shows us more convincingly how to look beyond local events and rebuild our lives according to universal values that should guarantee a sense of purpose and underwrite happiness. The later novel is sometimes described as 'more balanced' or 'more perfect' (sic) than the earlier one, but since life itself is far from being balanced or perfect, that very judgement seems to hand the palm to *War and Peace*.

Breakdown and Confession

You will know you have reached a dangerous existential crisis when you find yourself hiding all tools of possible self-destruction in order to avoid committing suicide on impulse. This was a point reached in the life of Levin at the end of *Anna Karenina* (Eight, 9), also by Tolstoy in real life just before that, and it will be referred to again in his next major work. The idea of suicide, encouraged and sustained in him by one philosopher above all others, was something he struggled with over a long period. The two years that followed the completion of his latest novel were not easy to live through. Still seeking help from religion, he went to church regularly, and spent long hours in solitary prayer. But everyone noticed how subdued he had become, lacking all confidence and *joie de vivre*. The spiritual agony was just about containable, but it did not diminish, and there was only one way to come to terms with it. At the age of fifty he had to go back over his life, examining all his old religious and philosophical doubts, queries and decisions, and think them through to a new conclusion. Intellect, and the distraction of writing it all down, would see him through.

And in a sense it did. The result was one of his finest works, fictional or otherwise, *A Confession*, written in 1879–80 only to be banned in Russia, though it circulated in illegal copies, and it was first published in Geneva as late as 1884. This 25,000-word study has been properly described by Prince D.S. Mirsky as 'one of the

...d's masterpieces... one of the greatest and most lasting expressions of the human soul in the presence of the eternal mysteries of life and death'.

The title could be confusing since it has commonly been used (sometimes in the plural) at the head of a mere autobiography, real-life or fictional. (See Rousseau, De Quincey, Musset, Mann, et al.) Tolstoy's work is generically different, being much closer to St Augustine's *Confessions*, which preceded him by a millennium and a half (AD 397–401). Augustine's was the first autobiography that had, as its primary purpose, not reminiscences or self-justification but *introspective analysis of the author's spiritual experience*. This applies equally to Tolstoy's confession, which tells the story of the writer's departure from the Orthodox Church in which he had been brought up, and his eventual return to God many years later, albeit full of misgivings and provisos.

Yet, even with that distinction cleared up, all is not what it seems. Something that looks like a search for God is actually a duel with death. Plenty of people search for God without necessarily suffering from existential terror at the thought of their own mortality. But Schopenhauer had taught Tolstoy that life is an evil to be cured only by overcoming the will to live. Not surprisingly, death now dictates everything he does, thinks and says. In the fourth chapter of *A Confession* he clearly describes death and annihilation as the only truth. His object in writing is to find a way of avoiding suicide and living with that truth. God is his means to that end, but death is the cause of the quest.

The way that he goes about his search in this work is paradoxical, and, yet again, misleading. At first sight it seems to be cerebral and schematic, along the formulaic lines of the little green stick of Tolstoy's childhood and the forty-two rules of his late youth. This attempt to penetrate beyond the obvious is a work of the rational mind, a gathering together of all Tolstoy's formidable intellectual powers in order to bring them to bear on the deepest of all mysteries. Measured out with almost mechanical calculation, this work is divided into two matching halves, a journey away from faith that lasts for eight roughly equal chapters, and a return trip that lasts for a similar space. (This overall binary shape is curiously similar to that of the Book of Ecclesiastes in the Old Testament, which is liberally cited in Chapter 6. We shall have more to say about this work below.) The language is simple, commonsensical, almost colloquial, and controlled by undeviating logic. He uses lists, programmes, arithmetical formulae. He eschews rhetoric or any fancy flourishes. But two things are slightly wrong with this. First, it seems inappropriate to bring algorithmic reasoning to bear on problems of spirituality. A surgeon does not use a plumber's tools. How can you pin down the meaning of life with forthright intellectualism? Reason can only undermine faith, never justify it. Secondly, as if to prove the point, at key points he deviates from this method in a most striking manner by turning repeatedly to colourful examples taken from legend, story, poetry and fable. Soon after illustrating a point by showing that $1,000 = 1,000$ or listing a brief argument a), b), c), d), he will launch into parable about a hungry beggar or the plight of a man sailing downstream out of control. The best story of all is an eastern fable telling of night and day, life and death, human destiny. A traveller hides in a well to escape a ferocious beast, but there, below him, is a dragon with open jaws. Unable to move up or down, he grabs a branch and holds on, though he can feel his grip getting weaker. When he looks round he sees two mice, one white, one black, eating away at his bush. He is doomed in all directions. But when he spots a few drops of honey on the leaves he licks them up. Such is life. This allegory, like several others, provides lively entertainment while serving his cause. Naturally enough, given the subject matter, excursions like this turn out to be more effective and memorable than any amount of studious argumentation. Tolstoy has made a deliberate attempt to press into service two quite different methods of persuasion and run them in double harness.

The subject matter is his personal biography, but only in so far as it concerns his religious attitudes. Tolstoy takes us through his life, describing how he abandoned religion and sought fulfilment through the possibilities open to any young man with ability – sensual pleasure including all the vices, soldiery, a literary career, travel, teaching, journalism, marriage and family life. Nothing gave lasting satisfaction; everything led to deepening disillusionment. Faced with the idea that the only thing to do with a human existence was to end it, Tolstoy turned for guidance to the great thinkers of the past, but found them unhelpful; they seemed to emphasise only the futility of it all. His chosen representatives of thinking humanity are an interesting little group: Socrates, Solomon, Buddha and – the only philosopher from modern times – Arthur Schopenhauer. Friends and neighbours were of no help, since they all belonged to one of four categories: the ignorant, the hedonistic, the suicidal, or the cowardly. He may not have used that term for the fourth category, but it is what he meant, because it included people who knew that life was a stupid joke but lacked the decisiveness to end it. Tolstoy had no reluctance in assigning Schopenhauer himself to this group.

The authenticity of this search for meaning and truth in the face of death stands beyond all question. No one has ever found an iota of exaggeration, self-dramatisation or self-pity in the agonising revelations of *A Confession*. This is compulsory reading for all thinking people with an interest in what transcends materialism, though they will need to be well stocked with antidotes to the poison of Schopenhauer that seeps onto almost every page. As for the author, at any stage his bleak negativism might have been relieved or even neutralised by half an hour of Mozart, a few lines from Pushkin or a glance at the behaviour of a puppy, but when you are determined to negate the value of living you must remain selective in your authorities and examples. A distillation of ideas taken from Plato, Epicurus, Boethius and Kierkegaard would have led to more reassuring conclusions. It is a pity also that Tolstoy lacked an adviser like P.G. Wodehouse's Jeeves, who warned Bertie Wooster off a similarly dark philosopher, substantially inspired by Schopenhauer, with the wise words, 'You would not enjoy Nietzsche, sir. He is fundamentally unsound.'

This work shows Tolstoy to have been wilfully determined to argue the pessimistic view of our condition, whatever the evidence. A good example comes to mind in the sixth chapter. Not only is his choice of thinkers suspect in itself, but the way he treats them tells the same story of accentuating the negative. For instance, his choice of Solomon as a thinker of major significance is unusual, and full of distortions. Tolstoy's citation of the famous words, 'Vanity of vanities. All is vanity!' is from the opening of the book of Ecclesiastes in the Old Testament. This was not written by Solomon, as even Tolstoy half admits by ending his long quotation with the words, 'So said Solomon, or whoever wrote those words.' But that is not important; what matters more is Tolstoy's tendentious use of the material from Ecclesiastes. This book is anything but an outright pessimistic rejection of human life. The first half (Chapters 1–6) certainly points out the vanity of all human achievement, but the last chapters (7–12) give us a good idea of how we can deal with this knowledge by acknowledging the goodness of living and the many possibilities of pleasure, if they are kept under reasonable control. As one commentator puts it, Ecclesiastes 'presents a running dialectic: the "vanity of things" being set over against the goodness of life'. The same writer sums up the achievement of this superb work by informing us that it offers 'an intellectually valid answer to the problem of existence'. But that was not what Tolstoy was looking for. He clearly did not read to the end, or if he did, he chose to suppress the actual message of the book. Either way, his choice of material is false and misleading in the way that he has dealt with it. There is more passion than logical thought in this example of his persistence with pessimism.

How could Tolstoy get out of this morass? The resolution of the dilemma is that already provided by the endings of his two first novels and also by the third one, which lay nearly twenty years in the future. It is argued out steadily over the latter chapters of *A Confession*, but the conclusion is fairly straightforward, if difficult to achieve: what you need is faith, acceptance, altruism and love. A concept of God must be accepted, though not the God of the established churches. God is good, God is the life force, God is love. What it amounts to is the best of Jesus without his church. This, at last, was something he could attempt to live by.

Achievements in an Eventless Life

It may seem ungracious to lump together the last three decades of a great man's life into a single entity for generalised consideration, but this can be justified in the case of Leo Tolstoy. When Leonard Woolf says, 'The story of this eventless life is infinitely more fascinating than that of a Napoleon, a Casanova, or a Livingstone. The reason is mainly in Tolstoy himself,' he is surely referring not to the first five decades (which included danger on the battlefield, foreign travel, marriage and the writing of two great masterpieces), but to the period of almost exactly thirty years that preceded his death on 7th November 1910.

This period is so lacking in 'events' that biographers compiling a brief reference chronology of the great man's life are reduced to singling out a letter to the Tsar as the major excitement of 1881, a walk from Moscow to Yasnaya Polyana as the big occurrence of 1886, and 'Renounces meat, alcohol and tobacco' as the most interesting detail of 1888 (and so on). Instead of tracing the small incidents of this life as and when they came about, it will be more useful to consider the main people that he had dealings with during this period, the main works that he wrote, his growing status as literary genius and guru, the development of his moral and spiritual preoccupations, and the state of his family affairs, especially his marriage.

The change that came over this author in terms of what to write and why he was writing can hardly be overstated. Halfway through *War and Peace* he took time out to castigate an aspiring young writer for whom the novel as a genre seemed to be 'a sugar coating to make the ideas of the author palatable'. At that time Tolstoy's own view was that a novelist should have no other aim than to make people laugh and cry, and love life; by this means he might dare to hope that his works would still be read by the next generation. A.N. Wilson's comment is apt: 'There is such sunny common sense in all of this that we might wonder how he could ever have come to abandon such a position.' But he did. After the conversion described in *A Confession* nothing could be the same. Religion and ethics would dictate everything he did, as man, thinker and writer. There was no point in writing without a moral purpose; didacticism was not only permissible, it was everything.

First of all Tolstoy satisfied his urge to write by continuing a series of simple tales for young people, though they were also enjoyed by older people who could only just read. They contained a straightforward idea: life is not worth living unless it is dedicated to goodness and God. In 'Two Old Men' (1885) a pilgrim on his way to Jerusalem never gets there because he stops on the way to help out a poor family and set them on their feet, but he is shown to be a better man than his friend, who continued the pilgrimage and visited every sacred place in the Holy Land. The latter pilgrim learns his lesson in the closing words: 'But he now understood that the best way for a man to keep his vows to God and to do His will is to show love and do good to others while he alive.' In a similar vein, 'Where Love Is, God is' (also 1885) tells the story of a cobbler who waits patiently for God to visit him, as promised in a dream, and performs three good deeds while he does so. At the end of the day, before he has time to feel disappointed that God never turned up, he opens his Bible to read the words, 'Inasmuch as ye have done it unto one of the least of these my brethren, ye have done it unto me.' The parable ends with the usual clear message: 'And Martin understood that his dream had come true, and that the Saviour had really come to him that day, and he had welcomed him.' The story entitled 'How Much Land Does a Man Need?' (1886) has a stronger narrative line: a grasping landowner, who can gain all the land he can run round in a day, expires from overexertion under a burning sun, and thus discovers the sad truth that all the land he needed was a six-foot plot.

These educational tales are modest masterpieces, picking up the forms and rhythms of the folk tales and parables on which several of them are based. The moral grows right out of the story, and the story is always recounted with great skill. They make a sharp impact, and are likely to be instantly memorised. Their artistic (and perhaps spiritual) power was brought home to the present author twenty years ago when a middle-aged lady wrote in to ask for identification of a tale she had heard dramatised many years before. She thought the title was something like 'The Three White Sages of the North'. 'There the three lived in simplicity, great solitude and Holy innocence...' She was able to give some details, and she recalled that, 'It was a tale told in language of distinction.' It turned out to be 'The Three Hermits' (1886), and we can safely allow this perceptive lady (who bore the angelic name of Gabriel) to sum up its quality:

What surprises me is how little, in terms of circumstance, I managed to retain of the story, and yet how lasting is its flavour, which was the clue... Then there are the cadences of style which mark it out. Even through the distortions of memory and translation, of being transformed into an early radio dramatisation, a distinct essence comes through. This says something about Tolstoy, and his power to make himself heard beyond his generation.

Here speaks a sophisticated intelligence; we can only imagine the effect these tales must have had on many a young mind or uncultivated personality. It is also sad to hear these words, Tolstoy's and the good lady's, because they seem to resonate from a lost age when it was deemed useful to demonstrate to young people, if not in church then certainly at school, the need for selflessness and love. How many children regularly hear messages like that in our modern secular society?

In this long, last period of his life Tolstoy's writings are prolific. Religion and politics obsessed him, especially the former. At one point (1882) he took time out to do to Hebrew what he had done to Ancient Greek a decade earlier, ingesting the language in a very short time in order to feel confident in translating the Old Testament. He kept up a ceaseless stream of articles, translations, letters, tracts, prefaces, replies, essays, sketches, open letters, appeals and exhortations. The general tone of these works is that of a hectoring preacher; they were described in America as 'utterances of such apostolic austerity that they read like encyclicals from the head of a great church – the church of humanity'. All the time he inveighed against the hypocrisy of the established Church in Russia, the iniquity of the Russian government, the immorality of *any* government or system of judgement, and of all property-owning, un-didactic art, military service and war, sexual activity, killing and violence of any kind, even defensive, all stimulants and almost all activities that brought people together in social groups that might run the risk of becoming exploitive. Although he never spelt out a positive programme, he seems to have stood for a primitive, anarchistic, agrarian society based on brotherly love, unaggressive and vegetarian, hard-working, with no division of labour (every man providing for himself), no money, no commerce, and presumably with little intercourse with other people at all. The astonishing thing is that this Rousseau-inspired farrago of well-intended but impractical principles was accepted by quite a number of adherents, who went so far as to form little colonies reserved for fellow-believers. True enough, his wife described most of the weird and scruffy worshippers who turned up at his gates as too crazy to be taken seriously, but most were sincere, all were well intentioned and many of them went away filled with inspiration to drop out of the modern world and live the good life.

The great man did not consider himself a Tolstoyan, however, and he denied the existence of Tolstoyism as a movement. He did not believe in special colonies, considering that if a man had any good in him he should spread the light as widely as possible. At some deep level he must have known that his own thinking was flawed, because although he preached brotherly love as the one force for salvation, he could never discover it in himself (misanthropy being his deepest well-spring), and he even admitted to an aspiring colonist in 1908 that such communities never lasted long because, once the 'external arrangement of life' had been arranged, every known example had collapsed because 'there began to be quarrels and gossip, and it all fell to pieces'. In the real world, pure fraternal love had to be acknowledged as an impossible dream. There could be no more accurate or succinct dismissal of the colony experiment, and it came from the master who inspired it.

The astonishing thing about this period is, given the self-imposed constrictions, its rich diversity. On the one hand we can read a half-page 'Introduction to Ruskin's Works' (1899), a few pages of 'Letters to Gandhi' (1910), or a short tract on the death penalty, 'I Cannot Be Silent' (1908). At the other extreme there are longer works running to hundreds of pages, like *What Shall We Do Then?* (1886), *The Kingdom of God is Within You* (1893) or *The Four Gospels Harmonised and Translated* (1881–2). But transcending them all is a series of literary works that ought not to be there at all because, although they all have a moral purpose, they were written to the highest standards of good storytelling and characterisation, those that had prevailed in this writer's best period of activity. They enjoy an artistic quality the like of which the master has theoretically repudiated, and, better still, there is no shortage of them. Half a dozen outright masterpieces belong to this period of literary and spiritual apostasy.

The Death of Ivan Ilyich (1886) is one of Tolstoy's finest achievements, a compressed and harrowing account of nothing less than dying and death, universally acknowledged as one of the finest stories ever written on this theme. The title and the beginning are unusual; together they announce the ending, the death of the main protagonist. Suspense has gone out of the window, and the positive effect of this is enormous: Tolstoy can get right into his subject and look closely at the sickroom and deathbed without risking an accusation of prurience. He does so relentlessly. The moral purpose of the story is clear. We are presented with a dying man who is forced to reconsider the way he has lived, and the obvious implication is that all readers should do the same thing and thus discover a better way of life. But here is the central irony that makes the story so strong and appealing. If Tolstoy had presented us with a villain, or at least a person with obvious faults that we could recognise as disgusting, the writer's moral purpose would have been distinct and unquestionable, though such heavy-handedness would also have deadened the intended effect. But Ivan Ilyich is not such a negative figure. His faults are run-of-the-mill and slight – he is materialistic, rather dull, complacent and more interested in playing cards with his friends than showing affection to his family – and we can at the least warm to him in his ordinariness. There is not an ounce of *schadenfreude* in the whole work. Because the dying hero is so like most of us in his mediocrity and limited vision we can feel unlimited sympathy for his undeserved affliction and untimely end. Where did Tolstoy, the ageing and impatient moralist, discover such reserves of objectivity and compassion?

Ivan Ilyich Golovin is a judge. The word *golova* means 'head' in Russian, which is a bad start because it announces starkly in advance what would be better learnt chapter by chapter, that this man is too cerebral, and insufficiently spiritual. Fortunately the nudge-nudge technique is immediately abandoned for good storytelling. We learn about Golovin's career, his innocent drift into marriage and acquisition of two children, and the little domestic accident which starts off his illness, which is probably cancer. (Physical trauma seems not to be a common cause of cancer, but this does not matter, and Tolstoy's antipathy to doctors was such that he would have been only too pleased to flout medical opinion.) The judge is under sentence.

He dies slowly and horribly after a long decline. It is an intense and moving story, brutally frank and directly concerned with the inevitability and nastiness of death, sparing us no unpleasant details of the anguish, the agony, the indignity of this man's condition. The narrative technique, much changed from that of the big novels, is devastatingly powerful. The style is terse enough to begin with, but as time goes on the chapters get shorter, as do the paragraphs and sentences. Everything shrinks down, compressing the narrative and crushing the sufferer until the conclusion, which brings greater relief than any other ending by this writer.

The moral of this work is not quite where Tolstoy intended it to be. *The Death of Ivan Ilyich* teaches a clearer artistic lesson than a spiritual one. If you tell a gripping story, present a balanced central character and restrain your didactic impulses, you may achieve a literary masterpiece, and if that happens your moral purpose will succeed more subtly and enduringly than if you had made your intentions clear beyond doubt.

A striking comparison comes immediately to mind. Only a couple of years later Tolstoy wrote a story on his second-favourite subject, sex. *The Kreutzer Sonata* (1889) is a shrill indictment of human sexuality. Once more the secret is out at the beginning. The narrator, on a train journey, meets a sullen individual, who turns out to be Pozdnyshev, a notorious killer found guilty of murdering his wife but freed because he claimed to have been defending his outraged honour in a *crime passionnel*. His victim was supposed to have been having an affair with a violin-playing visitor by the name of Trukhachevsky for whom Beethoven's Kreutzer Sonata was a favourite speciality. Since we know most of the main details at the outset, where is the interest supposed to lie? Only in Pozdnyshev's (and therefore Tolstoy's) extremely jaundiced view of sex. At the age of fifteen the future murderer visited a brothel, and had his first taste of sex with some now-forgotten woman, hastily and unfeelingly. This disgusting experience ruined him as far as natural physical relationships with women were concerned.

In the railway carriage Pozdnyshev fulminates against the widely sanctioned exposure of the female body, which, basically, was what tempted him into marriage, and also against honeymoons (licensed debauchery), the married state (which makes men 'incontinent'), as well as against himself and his jealousy, which was uncontrollable even before Trukhachevsky arrived and actually caused all the unhappiness. He insists that sex is at the root of all human misery, and it should be done away with – even if that means the extinction of the human species. And music should be done away with too since it causes most cases of adultery. (Tolstoy's attitude to music was painfully ambivalent: he was a good musician, who often played the piano, and music was one of his great loves, yet he mistrusted it as a dangerous force likely to release uncontrollable passions.) Pozdnyshev's lunatic diatribe goes on for twenty-eight senseless chapters, making this story half as long again as *The Death of Ivan Ilyich*. This piece is tedious, unsubtle, unrealistic and antihuman. And even the cheapest trick of all is transparently false; crazy notions are put into the mouth of a madman, as if to make them acceptable or excusable, but anyone who knows anything about Tolstoy will recognise these ideas as truly belonging to him. For example, in a letter to Chertkov written at the same time as this story his comment on sexual relations between husband and wife was, 'I think that for the good of mankind both men and women should strive for absolute chastity.' A work of absurdity, insulting to the intelligence and artistically inept, *The Kreutzer Sonata* is among the worst things ever to come from Tolstoy's pen, and it deserves nothing more than oblivion. This means nothing, however; permanently protected by his great name, a titillating reputation and a beautiful title, it is certain to survive.

First death and religion, then sex. Tolstoy's third preoccupation is with violence, and that subject was taken up in a work that occupied him over a long period, from 1896 to 1904, and was published posthumously in 1911. *Hadji Murat*, a tale of heroism in the Caucasus, is Tolstoy's last work that has a claim to greatness. He worked on it secretly, like an old man with a naughty book in the garden shed, because it was antithetical to all that he had written on the subject of pacifism. How could a devoted moralist waste so much time on a bloodthirsty historical adventure story? Tolstoy is fascinated with the murderous career of his hero, and obviously drawn to violence in an admiring way that contradicts his pacifist stance. More than that, he is prepared to acknowledge and demonstrate the *attractiveness* of going to war, the exciting appeal of fighting that works so powerfully on young men.

The beginning and the ending of this story contain the same image, that of a sturdy crimson thistle badly mutilated by a cart wheel but bravely refusing to surrender and die. This reminds the writer of a Caucasian hero who showed the same kind of courage when he was finally trapped and cut to pieces – a curious subject for admiration in a writer committed to non-resistance.

In 1851, when Tolstoy was serving as a junior officer in that region, Shamil had led the Chechen people in military resistance to the Russian invaders. But the local tribesmen, then as now, seemed just as interested in pursuing age-old feuds and rivalries among themselves. This story of vengeance and violence deals with the shifting alliances between Murat, Shamil and the Russians. We see them all, at rest and at prayer, preparing for action and fighting brutally on various fronts. Tolstoy's sympathies are evenly distributed between tribesmen, guerrilla leaders and ordinary Russian soldiers. This tale of only 35,000 words swarms with interesting characters, more than seventy of them named, including lots of real historical people, and many others in tiny passing roles, all of which gives the story an impression of amplitude comparable with that of *War and Peace*.

The finest quality of this work is the author's ability to infuse into his narrative many of his reforming ideas (sometimes expressed obsessively elsewhere), unemphasised and with apparent objectivity. The story comes first by a long way, and it could be read with excitement by anyone in any mood. But the more reflective reader will soon realise that it is not really possible to read this little novel without searching one's mind over a number of profound matters, some of them age-old questions of religion and philosophy, just the things that the author wants us to think about. The relationship between civilised man and nature; the wonderful phenomenon of the force of life that animates all of us; the ordering of attitudes to inevitable death; the effect of religion upon mentality and behaviour; the proper arrangement of moral standards; the universality of falsehood; the need for altruism; the all too easily suppressed instinct for brotherly love; the pleasant usefulness of family life; the propensity for those in government to misuse their power and become corrupt; the awful arbitrariness of nature and history; and, perhaps most obviously in this story, the ease with which men have recourse to violence, allowing it to become an enjoyable and honourable way of life and disregarding its horrific consequences – on all of these issues, and others, we are obliquely invited to form a judgement. For once, Tolstoy has not told us openly what conclusions to draw, he has not even asked direct questions, he has apparently set out his hidden arguments dispassionately, and yet *Hadji Murat* contains an inbuilt guarantee that a large majority of its readers, if they reflect at all, will sympathise with conclusions he has insisted upon elsewhere with greater, and unnecessary, stridency. A single page of this well-written story is more effective as a condemnation of cruel government and militarism than a trunkful of anarchist and pacifist pamphlets. Many people accept this work as Tolstoy's masterpiece in the post-*Anna Karenina* period.

One other story from this period, 'Master and Man' (1895), deserves a positive mention. This is a sophisticated and gripping adult example of the simple parables mentioned above. It reads like an amalgam of 'How Much Land Does a Man Need?' and *The Death of Ivan Ilyich*. Once again a greedy businessman, this time Vasily Brekhunov, sets off in risky weather conditions (a winter snowstorm) to pull off an advantageous land-deal. He takes a servant, Nikita, with him, and the two of them end up lost and in danger of dying in the snowy waste. At the last moment Brekhunov is blessed by a sudden vision of how wrong his life has been, and the need to redeem himself through an act of altruism and brotherly love. He covers Nikita's body with his own coat and then his own body, sacrificing his own life and saving another's. This bald summary does the tale no justice. There is enough subtlety in the tempting business deal, the convincing portraiture of the two men, the marginal feasibility of the journey, and the steady encroachment of the storm to keep the narrative interest vividly alive, and the ending, for all its open symbolism (Brekhunov dying in a Jesus posture with his arms extended), is powerful and moving.

Other Genres

We need to glance at a completely new genre for this writer. It is not as widely known as it should be that Tolstoy is an accomplished dramatist. We need not look at his early writing for the theatre, in the 1860s, which came to nothing of lasting value, but when he returned to the stage in the 1880s he suddenly produced one work which, despite displaying some of Tolstoy's didactic excesses, is so successful on the boards and so deeply disturbing that it has reached the international theatre, and stayed there in the repertory, still attracting audiences (albeit infrequently). It is hardly an exaggeration to describe this play, aptly entitled *The Power of Darkness* (1886), as the most successful tragedy in Russian literature, since that nation has no great tragic writer for the stage, and no heavyweight drama more impressive than this one.

This five-act story of Russian peasant life, first produced abroad and admitted to the Russian stage only in 1895, has an educative purpose. Tolstoy's aim was to draw attention to the disgusting primitivism of rural Russia decades after supposed reform, and while doing so proclaim a Christian message about the exponential infectiousness of evil behaviour. The weak-spirited Nikita Chilikin is manipulated by his wicked mother, Matryona, through a series of domestic atrocities that culminate in nothing less than infanticide (portrayed on stage). Eventually Nikita breaks down under the strain of events and confesses his crimes before the whole village community. A curious feature of the play is that it offers an alternative ending to the fourth act. For any director who might baulk at showing a baby being crushed to death, the author offers an alternative scene, in which the murderers are overheard recalling the crime.

A strong storyline and powerful action are the hallmarks of this play, which builds up a truly horrifying atmosphere in a steady crescendo of selfishness, greed, uncontrolled sexual desire and violence. The dialogue is conducted in strong Russian dialect speech, which needs to be reflected in any translation, however difficult that is to achieve. The structure is remorselessly logical, as in Classical drama, and the succession of personal crises, always growing in significance and intensity, are guaranteed to hold an audience in appalled fascination. Twenty-two characters represent all the ages of man from birth to sixty, and among them are three or four remarkable roles. Nikita is the very model of human susceptibility, and Matryona is all too convincing in the violent depravity that drives her on. Akim, her husband and polar opposite, is a small triumph of characterisation. He attempts to prevent or offset the evil actions with good words based on his Christian faith. This might have seemed simplistically pious if the author had not had the clever idea of giving the old chap a stammer, which makes his well-intended utterances endearingly comical and only half-understood. But all the time they are making steady preparation for the final scene of his son's confession. However unlikely it may seem, *The Power of Darkness*, which is founded on real events in a Russian village, has proved strangely successful in achieving something close to *Macbeth* with repentance in the last act. This is, through Tolstoy's art, the power of enlightenment.

Towards the end of his life Tolstoy made two extended pronouncements on culture that are largely ignored nowadays, but we need to note them in passing because they are historically significant, and they demonstrate the old man's extremist opinions and lack of common sense. Regrettably, we cannot conveniently ignore them. In 1897–8 he wrote a treatise on aesthetics under the title *What is Art?* For a short time, and by some people, it was taken seriously. George Bernard Shaw called it 'beyond all comparison the best treatise on art that has been done by a literary man... in these times'. This could only have been said by an individual who shared its narrow, utilitarian view of artistic endeavour and achievement. It is significant that Shaw, a follower of Marx and Henry George, was personally sympathetic to Tolstoy's blend of communism, socialism and religion. Most people, then as now, would bridle at any theory of art that rejects Shakespeare, Dante, Goethe, Bach, Beethoven, Raphael, Michelangelo, and almost all the acknowledged masterpieces in our libraries, concert halls and galleries (including Tolstoy's own great novels). This sort of thing gives iconoclasm a bad name, but it is what Tolstoy seriously proposed. He considered that art was not free to do what it wanted; it must be contained and directed by educational purpose. Art that is restricted in its appeal is dismissed as decadent, and independent beauty is of no consequence. Art can be justified only if it communicates universal emotions of an uplifting moral and religious character. It is effective only if it extends beyond educated people to inspire the simplest of minds with a vision of man's place in the world and relationship with God. The best that can be said for this artistic creed is that a generation later it became a kind of framework for Socialist realism in the writer's own country, though this, of course, was atheistic. The theory does not have many followers in the twenty-first century.

What is Art? was seriously discussed in its day, and still gets republished. This cannot be said of an absurd essay on the theatre, written by Tolstoy in 1903, 'Shakespeare and the Drama', best described by one recent critic as 'a headlong argument from false premises' and another as 'fifteen thousand words of nonsense'. Based on a reductionist analysis of *King Lear*, the argument proposes that all of Shakespeare's characters are unreal, they go about speaking an artificial language, and the plots in which they operate are derivative, unbelievable nonsense without any purpose or message. Even Shaw, who at first saw some sense in this – he, too, thought that Shakespeare's humanistic plays were deficient in moral guidance and philosophical consistency – soon rejected Tolstoy's extreme position on the grounds of Shakespeare's convincing characterisation and enchanting poetry. Thus the one distinguished contemporary who might have offered support for this crazy diatribe fell a long way short of being able to do so.

Tolstoy's volatility and contradictory nature emerge at this stage of his career as clearly as at any other time. While working on this silly piece, he not only continued to write *Hadji Murat*, a true masterpiece, but also dashed off, in a single day, a memorable story of five thousand words, 'After the Ball' (1903). The sharp impact of this short work derives from the contrast between two aspects of the same personality. An elderly colonel is first seen dancing with his daughter and charming the company, only to reappear the next morning enthusiastically directing the beating of a young soldier that is certain to result in his death. Needless to say, the narrator's love for this man's daughter does not survive this ghastly experience. It is remarkable how the same writer could so easily write with distinction and descend to the depths of inanity almost without recharging his pen.

Tolstoy's Resurrection

Many people simply do not know that Leo Tolstoy wrote not two long, serious novels, but three. The last one, *Resurrection*, is less famous than *War and Peace* or *Anna Karenina*, which is understandable. The earlier novels are not easy to emulate; who else has equalled them? But Tolstoy's last novel, after basking for a few years in the notoriety of its scandalous content, has fallen into neglect, and is now seriously undervalued. *Resurrection* is nowhere near the length of its distinguished predecessors, though it is one-third the length of *War and Peace* and two-thirds that of *Anna Karenina*. But there is more to this work than size. It has stories, characters and ideas written by a proven master whose narrative powers are still phenomenally strong.

A dozen years before its completion Tolstoy was told a remarkable story by a specialist in criminal law, A.F. Koni. One of this man's clients, called to jury service, had recognised the defendant in his first trial, a shabby prostitute charged with theft. Years before, Koni's friend had seduced a sixteen-year-old house servant, and abandoned her to her pregnancy and dismissal from service. Now here she was, a wreck of a woman whose downfall had been determined by him and his young lust. After playing his part in finding her guilty, he was overcome with remorse, and obtained permission to marry her. Alas, before he could begin to expiate his sin, she died in prison from typhus.

This remarkable story held a personal meaning for Tolstoy because of his own history of seducing young women from the peasantry and domestic staff. With Koni's blessing he decided to write it up as fiction, but the novel was nowhere near completion even ten years later. It needed a special impulse to make him finish the task, and this came in 1898 when he was presented with an urgent need for funds.

This arose because of a change in the destiny of a centuries-old religious sect known as the Dukhobors ('Spirit-fighters'). Tolstoy warmed to these people because they shared many of his personal beliefs, particularly in regard to pacifism, the immorality of property-ownership and the wrongness of eating animals. The Russian government was tightening its grip following the assassination of Alexander II in 1881, and repressive measures were taken against the Dukhobor community in 1895 because of their refusal to do military service. Immunised against government reprisals by his international reputation, Tolstoy supported their cause and signed every letter and manifesto supporting the Dukhobors.

Nicholas II offered a compromise. The Dukhobors would be allowed to leave the country en masse; land had even been found for them in North America. The only problem was how to pay for the transportation of seven thousand adherents. This was where Tolstoy came into the picture. Years before, he had renounced the copyright to all his literary works; now he reasserted his rights over his present writings in order to sell them at the highest possible price in Russia and abroad. His new novel was sold to a publisher for twelve thousand roubles, every kopeck of which went to the Dukhobor fund. But how would this novel, apparently churned out for financial gain, survive the self-imposed strictures of a man who was now more committed to ethical and religious instruction than to good storytelling?

Resurrection is Tolstoy's most controversial work. Nothing else written by him has excited such extremes of denigration and approval. Its worst misfortune is not to have been *War and Peace* or *Anna Karenina*. We have been reminded by every critic that this novel is not up to their standard. But isn't this like blaming *The Tempest* for not being *King Lear*? This novel, considered in its own right, stands out as a remarkable achievement and an unforgettable work. From the very first, opinion was divided over the merits and demerits of this novel. It was savaged by many critics of the day for its 'squalid sensuality' and 'satirical blasphemy', but it was also praised for its castigation of a vicious regime, and for its narrative strength. This debate has gone on, with diminishing intensity, for a hundred years.

If the more obvious demerits of the novel, lubricity and blasphemy, seem to have faded away, its qualities surely project themselves more clearly. It contains episodes of harrowing intensity, to say nothing of a hundred absorbing characters, from the inner group of realistically drawn people to a large outer circle of unforgettable Dickensian personalities. And the ideas in the novel, driving deep down beyond the reach of Dickens, will invite the reader to reconsider primary issues that seem to have been resolved in modern society, but have not. These concern judgement, the law, the medical profession, retributive action including imprisonment and the death penalty, and, in a broader sense, the distribution of wealth across society.

Prisons and prisoners are the main preoccupation of the novel, providing the setting for almost half the chapters. Tolstoy knew his subject well, having made numerous prison visits, enough to come away with a memory that remained strong and nauseating – the stinking physical atmosphere made worse by the stench of injustice. Most of the details came from personal knowledge and experience, or from newspaper reports and assiduous research. This accounts for the authenticity of so many chapters in his novel. There may be over-insistence in Tolstoy's presentation of this subject – in a couple of chapters Nekhlyudov ruminates too openly on the prison question – but there is no inaccuracy or exaggeration.

The story is compelling. No reader could be indifferent to the fate of the hapless Katerina Maslova, wrongly charged with murder, or that of the many friends and fellow-inmates who come into the story on her skirts. Will the injustice of the case against her be exposed and accepted? (Part One.) Will the next lawyer, senator, adviser, minister, prison-governor or well-placed contact be able to help Nekhlyudov sort things out? (Two.) What will happen to all the secondary characters that we have come to know so closely, sharing their misfortunes? (Two and Three.) Will the petition to the tsar be accepted? (Three.) Who will Maslova marry at the end? (Tolstoy experimented with several possible endings.)

Besides which, many of the most powerful scenes in the novel are not set inside a prison. A number of them are as good as anything you will find elsewhere in Tolstoy's work: the trial scene (occupying long stretches of Part One); the seduction of Katyusha (One, 16 and 17, the latter chapter having been censored out of some early editions); the preceding Orthodox Easter service at midnight (One, 15); Katyusha's desperate attempt to catch Nekhlyudov's attention as his train stops at night in their village (One, 37); Nekhlyudov's sadly amusing attempts to give land away to his suspicious peasants (Two, 2, 7, 9); a skirmish in the column of marching prisoners when a brutal guard insists on separating a convict from his tiny daughter (Three, 2); the double execution scene as recounted by the prisoner, Kryltsov (Three, 6). The authenticity of the central characters in *Resurrection* is underwritten, as usual, by the story's origin in real-life events and also by Dmitri Nekhlyudov's closeness to Tolstoy himself. More unexpected is the portrayal of a long succession of minor characters who float into the story and quickly depart. They crop up naturally enough because at times this novel reads like a picaresque adventure as the main protagonist wends his way through the whole of Russian society from the very top, including a meeting with a government minister, down to the lowest dregs, taking in the Church, the Army and the Law as he does so.

Tolstoy uses these short-lived characters for a double purpose. They have their natural role in the story, but the author also wants them to serve as satirical examples of some aspect of society that needs to be castigated, usually in connection with the law, the prison system or the civil administration of Russia. This is rather a dangerous thing to do – we do not want a line of silly caricatures testing belief beyond its limits. How does Tolstoy manage, with such economy, to establish a collection of believable people, connect each of them to a single idea and yet ensure that they remain recognisably human? The answer lies in a curious new formula invented for the purpose.

This has its basis in a quality for which Tolstoy is not particularly famous – humour. Time after time a minor character enters the story, establishes a clear position and a special significance, and is then softened, mellowed or enlivened by a mannerism or attitude that may not be funny in itself but is certainly so in its context. A judge is seen incongruously working out with dumb-bells before the session begins. One of his assistants, a superstitious man, counts his own steps as he walks into court and, needing a total that divides by three, cheats by skipping in a stride that isn't really there. Nekhlyudov visits an old general who enjoys great personal power in Petersburg, but we first see him ludicrously involved in contact with Joan of Arc over an Ouija board. A senator endlessly stuffs his prodigious beard and whiskers into his mouth and champs on them. Sometimes the humour darkens, as when a general gets the White Cross for what amounts to mass murder, and a department head caught out in criminal activities is rewarded by a governorship (admittedly in Siberia). But even these two bleak examples show how successfully Tolstoy uses irony to reveal aspects of character different from the persona exhibited by people in public.

This half-hidden comic technique extends throughout the novel, lightening the overall tone, and disguising the didactic spirit, all of which throws the numerous scenes of brutality into even sharper relief. The characters themselves are not diminished by their satirical function; they may look a bit silly, but they are made to seem like real people with human foibles rather than the embodiment of Tolstoy's ideas that they could have been. They are shown doing a lot of harm, and missing opportunities for good, but by no means all of them are wicked men and women – much of the blame lies in the systems and practices they have to work with.

Dmitri Nekhlyudov appears in four works by Tolstoy: *Boyhood* (1854), 'A Landowner's Morning' (1856), 'Lucerne' (1857) and *Resurrection*. He is also in several respects a literary incarnation of the author himself. These five manifestations of one character have a good deal in common, not all of it positive. In all of them we see the same person, a well-intentioned, thinking individual unafraid of the unconventional, full of moral sensitivity and eager to change the world. But it is equally obvious that there is an obnoxious side to this personality, who suffers from an excess of self-certainty and self-dramatisation. The man who wants to change things because humanity is so awful is himself corrupted by self-interest. (Further echoes here of Jean-Jacques Rousseau.)

There is something awkward about Nekhlyudov, and it begins with his name, which marks him out in negative terms. Its meaning suggests that he is an outsider, somehow 'not for people' (*ne k lyudyam*). We cannot begin to guess what antisocial traits his ancestor may have displayed to merit such a name, but something of them has come down to our modern man, whose stock-in-trade is unsociability. And Tolstoy knew this at the outset, having picked this name when he was twenty-seven years old for a callow character of only sixteen summers. When the mature Tolstoy saw fit to resurrect both the character and the name forty-odd years later, this decision cannot have been without meaning.

This remarkable continuity of characterisation, over several works and nearly half a century, has had one beneficial effect on the novel. It underlines Nekhlyudov's consistency. This man was fully outlined by his mid-teens and remains undeviatingly true to himself throughout his long story. Nekhlyudov (behaving like Tolstoy himself) cuts himself off from humanity, bit by bit, person by person, class by class, until he is marooned on an island of self-righteous pride. He has lived up to his name, being 'not for people'.

The saddest thing about Nekhlyudov (as with Tolstoy) is the triumph in him of rage over good sense. Here we have a person of acute perception and undeniable moral quality, who wishes to change human affairs for the better. But why does he have to be so misanthropic and pessimistic? (The astonishing thing about human activity is not that it sometimes reverts to brutality, but that this is uncommon, most people having an instinct for civilisation and generosity.) In his impatience that the world is so imperfect, why does he have to direct such fury against those who will not come into line and work dramatically to put things right in an instant? What right does he have to assert that the entire legal and penal systems must be instantly dispensed with rather than that incremental improvements be insisted upon, leading to a better future world? It was this kind of well-intended unworldliness that would eventually ensure the demise of every Tolstoyan colony that ever arose.

But these thoughts are misleading. Great credit still goes to the author and the hero. In this novel they will captivate all readers in a series of unforgettable events and characters, and they have stirred up a debate about Crime and Punishment (which would have been an excellent title for this work) that has not yet run its course.

Marriage in Decline

The story of the Tolstoys' marriage, towards the end, is nothing less than horrible and catastrophic. When he eventually ran away from home in the middle of the night, at the age of eighty-two, only to collapse and die at a railway station, his main purpose seems to have been to get away from the pressure of people, from his disciples and worshippers on the one hand, but also from his own family, and especially his wife. He had considered running away from her several times before, and now he could stand no more. After his death she admitted to a sense of guilt over this, knowing she had driven him away and probably precipitated his death. How did the marriage that began so well forty-eight years before descend to these abysmal depths of acrimony?

The first signs of disharmony may not have been much different from those between all couples whose married life extends into decades; over-familiarity, impatience and a little bickering are not uncommon in the best of unions. But a noticeable change for the worse occurred as the great writer emerged from his spiritual crisis, determined to live a different kind of life. It was Tolstoy who deepened the discord between them as early as 1882 by drawing attention to the disparity between his family's relatively luxurious lifestyle and the primitive way he thought everyone ought to live. This caused him great agony. On the one hand, his supporters, and his detractors, encouraged him to give up everything and live the simple life along with his dependants. On the other, his wife had an estate to run and many mouths to feed; she could see no sense in pointless deprivation and futile gestures. Tolstoy was torn apart by a continuing love for his wife which conflicted with his deepest principles. If she had been submissive all might have been well, but Sofya was still capable of resisting him. She noted a growing coldness on his part, and heard for the first time that he was tempted to run away from them all. It was not easy for her to understand the niceties of moral purity when nursing a sick child in the middle of the night with her husband absent. It has been claimed that in these early days of profound discord, twenty years after their happy union, we can see the first signs of mental instability on Sofya's part; certainly she began to threaten suicide at this time. She, in return, began to wonder about her husband's state of mind. When a happy man suddenly sees only what is terrible in life and shuts his eyes to what is good, does he not need some medical or psychological attention?

The differences and the animosity that existed between them could not be kept secret. Plenty of people noticed, and commented. Disciples of Tolstoy sympathised with him so profoundly that they were setting up the first colonies for people to try and live together according to his radical principles. At the same time, most objective outsiders were sorry for Sofya, who had to go on from year to year, witnessing her husband's agonies and following the development of his ideas. They could see why she was driven ever further into her own extremist position; it is no exaggeration to say that she came to loathe his teaching and its consequences. And yet, throughout the 1880s, in all other respects, we are told, they remained 'a model couple'. Temporary reconciliations were certainly achieved, and sometimes they lasted for months on end, but the deep breach between them was unbridgeable, and would only get wider.

While she did her best for her family, Tolstoy, urged on by disciples, went from one moral reform to another. For several years he had abandoned narrative literature in favour of religious tracts and simple moral stories. He travelled up and down, calling at monasteries, living in Moscow, sometimes in the slums, going all the way down to the Crimea, always conscious of people who were suffering, especially from famine relief and urban deprivation. He gave up his aristocratic title, and refused to do jury service. He worked in the fields and made shoes for his daughters. He gave up hunting and smoking, became a vegetarian, fathered more children and saw one of them die, founded a temperance society and suffered badly from erysipelas (a skin disease that turns the face bright red, a noticeable disfigurement in the portraits of the older Tolstoy). At home the atmosphere crackled with tension, and the simplest occurrence, like the serving of food slightly at variance with the new principles, often resulted in a violent outburst from him, followed by a dreadful row. One of the many things he objected to was the use of money. In his case this was manageable because he hardly used it anyway, but his leading disciple, Vladimir Chertkov, who shared this attitude, brought ridicule upon the Tolstoy movement by ensuring that when he renounced the use of money his wife kept on signing cheques and his secretary went with him to buy tickets at the railway station.

In mentioning the name of Chertkov we have arrived at the third baleful figure in Tolstoy's life story, a most unpleasant person, an *éminence grise* with hypnotic charisma, who gradually prised Tolstoy away from his wife and took over his mind, reinforcing his well-intended principles with massive force and insisting on their fulfilment to the last letter, a character who must bear much of the blame for pushing his master's foolish radicalism into a wild and weird otherworldliness that makes his good intentions look absurd. The depth of Chertkov's influence can be measured against a comment made by a close family friend, endorsed and recorded by Ilya, Tolstoy's second son: 'Ever since that gentleman turned up [in 1883] I really don't know which of Tolstoy's works are by Tolstoy, and which are by Chertkov.'

When the two men met, Tolstoy was fifty-five and Chertkov twenty-nine, the latter having been converted to Tolstoy's way of thinking by reading the last section of *Anna Karenina* followed by *A Confession*. The affinity between them was instantaneous, profound and enduring. They met as often as possible and when they were apart they wrote long missives to each other. At least a thousand letters have survived. Their relationship has been described in terms of a love-match without the physicality. This idea must have occurred to his wife because in this context she reminded him of a diary entry which he had made the best part of fifty years before (29th November 1851), and which she had not forgotten: 'I have never been in love with women... I have often been in love with men.'

The devastating impact and increasing influence of Chertkov on the mind and behaviour of Leo Tolstoy can hardly be over-stated. What began as mutual admiration based on affinity turned into a process of domination and control exercised by the younger one over his elder. Before long Chertkov was telling Leo Nikolayevich what to write, how to write it and how to behave when he was not writing. On one occasion Chertkov even objected to the old man learning how to ride a bicycle, asking, 'Is this not inconsistent with his Christian ideals?' Henri Troyat puts the position plainly: 'Chertkov had campaigned energetically for the cause. His subjugated master had delegated virtually all his powers to him. Not one line by Leo Tolstoy could appear without his agent's imprimatur.'

Chertkov may have captivated everyone he met with his good looks and aristocratic charm, but there is a long catalogue of reminiscences which tell the true story of his character. For all his acceptance of Tolstoy's modified Christianity, with its emphasis on meekness, non-resistance and the need for love, he was an unscrupulous schemer, bad-tempered and quarrelsome, mesmeric and domineering (some said oppressive and tyran-nical) and quite hypocritical, especially in matters of property and money. Tolstoy's friend and translator Aylmer Maude said he never knew anyone with such a capacity for forcing his will on others. 'Everybody connected with him became his instrument, quarrelled with him, or had to escape.' A live-in Swiss tutor described him in these terms: 'He had all the essential attributes of a sectarian: the blind inflexibility in matters of doctrine, and the aridity, the stubbornness and crudeness, refusing to recognise any subtleties or shades, and the heartless indifference to human contingencies.'

We have heard this story twice before, and we face the same question. Why did this big strong genius of a man capitulate before the intellectual power and spiritual teaching of a monstrous personality? Once again, the answer lies at the negative end of human experience. Henri Troyat leads us in the right direction: Vladimir Chertkov became 'a cumbersome incarnation of Tolstoy's own conscience'. It is a question of self-lacerating remorse at his own failings. His readiness to obey Chertkov's strictures 'expressed the old man's eternal tendency to self-accusation. He had felt guilty all his life long.' Dmitri Levin, his literary alter ego, admits to something similar in *Anna Karenina*: 'The chief thing for me is not to feel guilty.' We are back where we started, with Tolstoy's youthful sense of self-disgust that he was so relieved to find confirmed in the works of Rousseau. He dived under Rousseau's wing in his teens, he summoned Chertkov to his deathbed (while excluding the woman who had been his wife for half a century), and for long stretches in middle life he was closely attached to Schopenhauer. Over the years these three misanthropists kept him resolute in the self-hatred that governed his attitude to humanity at large.

Chertkov went to England several times, and eventually for a long stay to avoid persecution at home, but he was allowed back into Russia three years before Tolstoy's death. He had a large and expensive house built (much to the chagrin of Tolstoy, who saw this as an infringement of their shared ideas about owning property and using money), and moved in only a couple of miles from Yasnaya Polyana, much to Sofya's horror since she viewed him with loathing and dread. By now the younger man had grown beyond his hero-worship of the early days, and worked his way into the position of chief adviser to his master. He and Sofya were at daggers drawn until the very end. Both of them and several family members were involved in a protracted and unseemly scramble over diaries, notes and wills, bringing Sofya to bouts of hysteria and paranoia. This is hardly surprising. A.N. Wilson reminds us that a young secretary described the atmosphere at Yasnaya Polyana in those dying days: 'Bulgakov notices the strands of sheer hatred which run through the whole situation. He recognised eventually that Chertkov was aiming at the "moral destruction" of Tolstoy's wife in order to get at his manuscripts.' His purpose was achieved in its last detail. The fact that Chertkov later dealt responsibly with the great man's literary estate cannot be seen as retrospective vindication of his cruel treatment of Sofya.

Eventually Tolstoy ran away from both of his persecutors, but they heard the widely broadcast news of his collapse, and both managed to get over to the station of Astapovo, where the old man had only a few hours to live. He was just conscious when Chertkov was admitted. Sofya was kept out, on the certain grounds that the sight of her would surely finish her husband off, and a Pathé newsreel cameraman has left us with an agonising sequence of film, which shows her dumpy figure standing pathetically on tiptoe as she strove to get a glimpse into the room from which she was excluded. Only when Tolstoy suffered a relapse and lost consciousness for good, did they allow her in to sit with him. She was there when he died, but he wasn't aware of it.

Afterlife

Leo Tolstoy had contemplated death on a daily basis, in the abstract and the particular, for the latter half of his long life. No one could have been better prepared for the end; he had thought it through in the last detail. For instance, in a diary entry from nearly ten years earlier he had proposed the following experiment to be conducted during his last hours:

> When I am dying I would like to be asked whether I still see life as... a growing towards God, an accumulation of love. If I can't speak, I'll close my eyes if the answer is yes, and I'll look upwards if it is no.

Everyone knew about this, but on the day no one thought to ask the question. The whole business of his dying was a ghastly shambles, with everything out of joint. The apostle of love had run away in a spirit of bitter malevolence. He had travelled by train and finished up at a railway station, having ceaselessly denounced railways for many years. He lay ill long enough to become surrounded by six doctors, a police chief, government officials and an elder from a nearby monastery, even though he had repudiated all the institutions they stood for. He was given artificial respiration and morphine even though he had specifically objected to this kind of intervention the day before. Even his English-language death notice went wrong.

A premature report of his demise was received in London, and *The Times* published its obituary on 17th November 1910, only to follow it with another one and an apology on 21st November. The man who had told us to love one another and to learn how to die well was not able to do either of these things himself. If we are to learn anything from his passing we can do so only by treating it as an object lesson in how not to love, how not to prepare for death, how not to die. This may seem sadly ironical, but, considering the paradoxes and contradictions of this man's life, it must have been both inevitable and appropriate for the god of inconsistency to be in at his death.

His body was taken to a small railway station at Zaseka, and carried aloft to the nearby Yasnaya Polyana estate. Thousands had turned up for the funeral, and there would have been thousands more if the government had allowed the extra trains that had been requested. The people crowded through the house, filed past the open coffin and gathered around the burial place selected by the great man – a small glade in the Stary Zakaz forest overlooking the ravine of the little green stick. The ceremony was a curious one. There were to be no religious rituals, partly because Tolstoy had not wanted any but also because the Church had refused any such possibility. And yet over the grave every heart was moved when hundreds of voices launched into a spontaneous rendering of 'Eternal Memory' from the Russian Orthodox funeral service, with everyone kneeling and praying, bare-headed. Sofya was there for the interment. Chertkov was not; he would not have been welcome, and his work on that estate was done.

The estate itself is now a literary museum of the highest quality, staffed by dedicated experts under the direction of Tolstoy's great great grandson, Vladimir. (The latest guidebook includes a complete list of Tolstoy's descendants, a scattered dynasty that now numbers nearly three hundred.) Tourists and visitors flock to Yasnaya Polyana in their thousands, seminars and conferences are held there all the time, and it is customary for brides to call in on their wedding day and leave flowers by the grave. The museum, founded in 1928, Tolstoy's centenary year, was overrun and wrecked by the Nazis during the Second World War, but fortunately all the main exhibits had been sent away beyond the Urals. The sacking of Bald Hills by Napoleon's passing regiments in *War and Peace* (Volume Three, Part Two, Chapter 5) can be read as a dreadful foreshadowing of those events. Today, however, meticulous restoration has ensured that a faithful impression has been preserved of the main buildings, including the house in which Tolstoy wrote most of his works.

The writings themselves have been given exceptionally thorough editorial treatment at home and abroad. In Russia the definitive, ninety-volume edition of the *Complete Works*, which we referred to at the outset, took more than twenty years to complete, at first under the direction of Vladimir Chertkov, though ironically it was based on versions approved by Tolstoy's wife, his bitterest enemy. Abroad, all other English translations were superseded by another Centenary Edition, the one translated and edited by Louise and Aylmer Maude, which took up many years, from 1929 to 1937. Astonishingly detailed and perceptive biographies have been written in English by Aylmer Maude, E.J. Simmons, Henri Troyat, A.N. Wilson and others. Tolstoy's letters and diaries have been translated and edited by R.F. Christian, who has also written definitively on *War and Peace*.

As far as Tolstoy's reputation is concerned, some things have changed but he is still a huge figure in human history. At the time, his death was marked as a sensational event more because of his ideas than as a result of his literary achievement. Seeing him primarily as a bitter opponent of the Russian government and the Orthodox Church, students, revolutionaries, non-conformists and religious extremists all over Russia and beyond warmed to him as a rebel and supporter of their cause. His didactic and moralising works had reached many more people than his finest fiction. But now that a century has passed his heavy pendulum has swung the other way. His ideas are noted and remembered by some, but his literature is deeply loved by many. Look him up in any literary companion and you are likely to see his works given status alongside Greek tragedy and Elizabethan drama. In this book we have mentioned or described more than forty works by Tolstoy; virtually all of them are still in print, several existing in multiple English versions. New translations, even of the longest works, continue to pour from the press. Dozens of his works have been filmed for the cinema or TV. This writer is truly established as one of the brightest luminaries in cultural history, and interest in his work shows no sign of flagging.

Huge amounts have been written on this voluminous subject, and you may think there is little more to be said. But there always is something. At the end of his work A.N. Wilson says of the great writer, 'The more evidence we possess about Tolstoy, the less he makes sense.' Since Wilson has spent much time examining the paradoxes and contradictions that surround his subject he must mean that even taking these into account there are still fundamental things that remain to be explained about Leo Tolstoy. Is there no guiding principle that will 'make sense' of this giant?

In an effort to provide an overall interpretation of Tolstoy's attitudes and behaviour that is consistent (though it can never be complete), we have sought to place more than usual emphasis on three relationships that partly reflected, but substantially controlled the course of Tolstoy's artistic and spiritual life from start to finish. At the risk of offending Tolstoy-lovers, especially in his homeland, where, naturally enough, he is treated with reverence, it must be stated plainly that these associations bring us to a disagreeable conclusion.

At the deepest level of his psyche Leo Tolstoy seems to have been an unhappy, unpleasant man attracted to other unhappy, unpleasant men through inescapable affinity. The four of them seem to attract and deserve each other. They can be imagined as a querulous quartet occupying their own small circle of Dante's Inferno, with no one else for company. In his innermost spirit Tolstoy seems to have hated himself and all humankind for our uncontrollable animal nature; he resented even being alive, and burdened himself with an insupportable feeling of guilt for the iniquity of us all. This made him, like his three masters, angry, intolerant and uncongenial; all four, in their intransigence, brought suffering and hatred into the lives of those closest to them. He was similar to them in his personal behaviour throughout his life – awkward, truculent, prickly. Even in the army, he regarded his fellow officers as coarse and vulgar, while they saw him as haughty and distant. Not for nothing did Turgenev call him a troglodyte in metropolitan society. In later years his unsociability grew into outright, aggressive enmity. It is this *negative* principle, in his personality, thinking and writing that makes overall sense of Leo Tolstoy, consistently explaining the man, his life, his conduct and most of his work. This may be said despite the magnificently optimistic anomaly created by *War and Peace*, which was written under the special circumstances described above. It is true that Tolstoy often has visions of brightness, and when he does he can communicate the goodness of living better than any other writer. But these are not consistent, nor do they accord with the general run of the man's life or his behaviour towards others. The Tolstoy of shining optimism, new Christianity, love of life and brotherly affection, is a hopeful theory, not the real Tolstoy. This is a man who could not respond to the genius of Shakespeare or Mozart, loathing the one and fearing the other. Instead, he clung to darker personalities, Rousseau, Schopenhauer and Chertkov, and his closeness to them defines him for us in heart, mind and body.

I have just checked with Yasnaya Polyana: Rousseau's medallion is long lost, but portraits of Schopenhauer and Chertkov are still there on the wall of Leo Tolstoy's small study. Even in the afterlife they brood over his captured spirit.

Bibliography

John Bayley, *Tolstoy and the Novel* (London, 1966)

Isaiah Berlin, *The Hedgehog and the Fox: an Essay on Tolstoy's View of History* (New York, 1966; London, 1967)

Harold Bloom (ed.), *Leo Tolstoy's 'War and Peace'* (New York, 1988)

T.G.S. Cain, *Tolstoy* (London and New York, 1977)

R.F. Christian, *Tolstoy's 'War and Peace': A Study* (Oxford, 1962); *Tolstoy: A Critical Introduction* (Cambridge, 1969); *Tolstoy's Diaries*, (2 vols, London, 1985)

Edward Crankshaw, *The Making of a Novelist* (New York and London, 1974)

Henry Gifford, *Tolstoy* (Oxford, 1982)

Malcolm Jones (ed.), *New Essays on Tolstoy* (Cambridge, 1978)

Janko Lavrin, *Tolstoy: an Approach* (London, 1944)

Derrick Leon, *Tolstoy: His Life and Work* (London, 1944)

Aylmer Maude, *The Life of Tolstoy* (2 vols, London, 1908–10; reprinted, Westport, Connecticut, 1970)

Donna Tussing Orwin, *Tolstoy's Art and Thought, 1847–1880* (Princeton, 1993)

Theodore Redpath, *Tolstoy* (London, 1960)

E.J. Simmons, *Leo Tolstoy* (Boston, 1946; reprinted New York, 1960)

George Steiner, *Tolstoy or Dostoevsky: An Essay in the Old Criticism* (New York, 1959; reprinted Harmondsworth, 1967)

Henri Troyat, *Tolstoy* (New York, 1967)

Edward Wasiolek (ed.), *Critical Essays on Tolstoy* (Boston, 1986); *Tolstoy's Major Fiction* (Chicago, 1978)

A.N. Wilson, *Tolstoy* (London, 1988; Harmondsworth, 1989)

Biographical Note

Professor A.D.P. (Tony) Briggs is a Russianist with other literary interests. A leading authority on Alexander Pushkin, on whom he has written several books and many articles, he has also specialised in Leo Tolstoy's life and career. His translation of *War and Peace* (Penguin Books, 2005) has sold 60,000 copies and achieved critical acclaim. It has been followed by new translations of *The Death of Ivan Ilyich, and Other Stories* (2008), and *Resurrection* (2009). His translations of Tolstoy's *A Confession*, and *What is Religion?* are published by Hesperus Press in 2009 under the title *A Confession*. He has also edited six volumes in the Everyman Poetry series, including translations from Pushkin. His definitive edition of the *Rubaiyat of Omar Khayyam*, (Orion Books, 2009) marks the bicentennial of Edward FitzGerald.

He is a Senior Research Fellow at Bristol University and Professor Emeritus at Birmingham University.

SELECTED TITLES FROM HESPERUS PRESS

Brief Lives

Author	Title
Andrew Brown	*Brief Lives: Gustave Flaubert*
Robert Chandler	*Brief Lives: Alexander Pushkin*
Melissa Valiska Gregory and Melisa Klimaszewski	*Brief Lives: Charles Dickens*
Patrick Miles	*Brief Lives: Anton Chekhov*

Classics and Modern Voices

Author	Title	Foreword writer
Anton Chekhov	*Three Years*	William Fiennes
Anton Chekhov	*The Exclamation Mark*	Lynne Truss
Fyodor Dostoevsky	*The Double*	Jeremy Dyson
Fyodor Dostoevsky	*The Eternal Husband*	Andrew Miller
Nikolai Leskov	*Lady Macbeth of Mtsensk*	Gilbert Adair
Vladimir Mayakovsky	*My Discovery of America*	Colum McCann
Alexander Pushkin	*Dubrovsky*	Patrick Neate
Alexander Pushkin	*The Tales of Belkin*	Adam Thirlwell
Leo Tolstoy	*The Forged Coupon*	Andrew Miller
Leo Tolstoy	*A Confession*	Helen Dunmore
Yevgeny Zamyatin	*We*	Alan Sillitoe

HESPERUS PRESS

Hesperus Press, as suggested by the Latin motto, is committed to bringing near what is far – far both in space and time. Works written by the greatest authors, and unjustly neglected or simply little known in the English-speaking world, are made accessible through new translations and a completely fresh editorial approach. Through these classic works, the reader is introduced to the greatest writers from all times and all cultures.

For more information on Hesperus Press, please visit our website: **www.hesperuspress.com**

ET REMOTISSIMA PROPE

MODERN VOICES